THE ART AND COLOUR OF GENERAL MOTORS

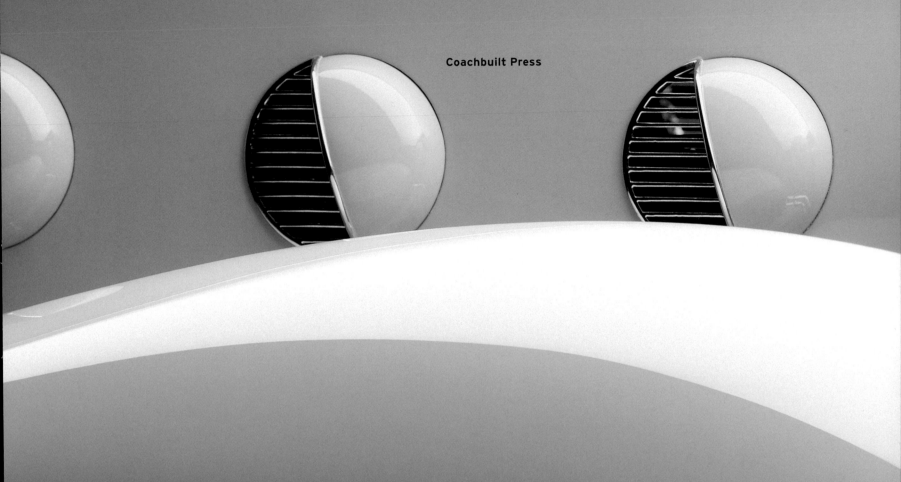

Coachbuilt Press

THE ART AND COLOUR OF GENERAL MOTORS

Foreword by
Bob Lutz

Introduction by
Nicola Bulgari

Essays by
Phil Patton

Terry V. Boyce

Michael Lamm

Edited by
Jonathan A. Stein

Design Commentary by
Stewart Reed

Photographs by
Michael Furman

Contents

Stewart Reed, automotive designer and
chairman of the Transportation Design
Department at Art Center College of Design,
offers his expert commentary throughout
The Art and Colour of General Motors.
He compares and contrasts the styling and
design elements as presented in the studio
photographs of Michael Furman. Mr. Reed's
initials (SR) will follow his comments.

Foreword
by Bob Lutz

The Art and Colour of General Motors is a remarkable work, the result of efforts by a number of talented writers, photographers, editors, graphic design artists and a host of others, who pooled their skills to produce this outstanding look at the history of General Motors Design.

Although I don't think we should live in the past when GM's best days are squarely in front of us, the images captured here, some for the first time, present a fantastic look at where we've been; some even hint at where we're going.

This book is a succinct history of the GM Design Department from its inception in 1927 to the present and includes essays from some of the world's most respected automotive journalists and historians. It tells the stories of luminaries like Harley Earl and such landmark designs as the classic Corvette, the new Camaro (a piece written by our own head of global design, Ed Welburn) and the once-ubiquitous tail fin.

For as long as I can remember, I have been passionate, enthusiastic and frankly obsessed with automotive design. Design is what sets a vehicle apart, what separates a good car from a great car. It's what creates enthusiasm for the automobile and sparks an emotional bond between car and customer. And it's the reason that the automobile inspires a passion among consumers like no other product, ever.

This book, in the way it artfully documents a spectacular past and hints at a fabulous future, has found a fan in this design devotee, and I'm sure it will make one of you, too.

Bob Lutz, Vice Chairman, Global Product Development, General Motors
Corporation and a veteran auto industry executive. A collector in his
own right, Mr. Lutz is a participant at the major concours and expositions
around the world.

Introduction
by Nicola Bulgari

I feel truly honored to be in the company of Mr. Lutz and Mr. Welburn as we celebrate the glorious history of General Motors Design. The styling of 1930s and 1940s GM automobiles has had a profound influence not only on my collecting passion, but on my life as a whole. Buicks and Cadillacs from that period sparked love affairs with both automobiles and America—love affairs that have continued to burn for 60 years!

As a child growing up in post-war Rome, late 1930s and early 1940s American cars—primarily Buicks, Cadillacs and Packards—captivated me. These were the cars of choice of important and wealthy people, Italian government agencies and the mainstay of the Vatican's papal fleet. Majestic and powerful, they left an indelible impression on me. They became my boyhood passion, my fantasy about life in America. I promised myself that when I grew up, I would own a big American car.

I learned as much as I could about American cars by collecting toy models and reading old copies of *National Geographic* that were filled with romantic automobile advertising. In the mid 1930s, Buick was one of the first American automobiles exported to Italy, and the one that initially captured my imagination and heart. It remains the nameplate I am most passionate about. Studying the artistic advertisements I also discovered that Buick, in the late 1930s, was a highly revered nameplate in China. Interestingly, it still is.

When I was seven or eight years old, I was seduced by a magnificent 1935 Buick 96S Sport Coupe I saw in an advertisement. With its long hood and flowing art deco lines, it was the most elegant car I had ever seen. It had such an impact on me that I fantasized about going to America and actually seeing a real one. I never forgot the fantasy.

Some 50 years later, I found one of the 41 96S coupes built by Buick: it was badly neglected, rusting away and needed everything. After a painstaking five-year restoration, we showed it in 2003 and won a trophy at Pebble Beach. It remains my favorite car, one I drive whenever possible.

Growing up in a family with over 100 years of involvement in hand-crafting precious metals and luxurious jewelry, I learned at a very early age to appreciate and understand masterpieces of design and how dreams are turned into reality. As a student of the automobile industry for more than half a century, I've also learned to appreciate the functional precision and beauty of mass-produced vehicles. I am attracted to the jewel-like qualities of Buick's LaCrosse and Enclave and Cadillac's CTS and XLR, vehicles I use for daily transportation in Italy and the United States.

My collection of American cars, which includes the 1938 Buick 90L Vatican escort car for Pope Pius XI and two Cadillac limousines used by cardinals, symbolizes my passion for preserving history and for sharing values instilled in me by my wonderful parents. Nothing gives me more pleasure than sharing my cars, − whether it be through a museum, a concours, or my collection, − to reunite Americans with the proud heritage of General Motors and the American automobile industry.

Congratulazione, General Motors, on going into your second century.

Nicola Bulgari is Vice Chairman of the Bulgari Group and has the world's largest private collection of vintage Buicks.

The Studio Approach
by Jonathan A. Stein

Like any great design or project to come out of a studio, *The Art and Colour of General Motors* started as a small idea that took a team to execute. With the idea of a spectacular book about General Motors anchored by the photographs of Michael Furman, co-publishers Furman and Richard Adatto engaged me to help them tell the story of 100 years of General Motors design.

Rather than select one author to write the book from a single point of view, in an effort to add richness, we assembled a team—much in the manner of how a great car takes shape in a modern studio. Each author was selected based on his particular talents and area of expertise. Some of the authors involved had worked with Coachbuilt Press before, while others joined us for the first time.

To chronicle the earliest days of GM, we invited writer and design historian Phil Patton to be part of the team, while former Campbell-Ewald writer, automotive journalist and historian Terry Boyce told the story of the first years of the Art and Colour Section and veteran automotive historian Michael Lamm brought alive the story of the Parades of Progress and Motorama. *Automobile Quarterly's* Tracy Powell, fresh from having written *General Motors Styling 1927-1958*, the tale of the tailfin, while *Corvette Quarterly's* Jerry Burton explained the genesis of the Corvette and GM's other two-seaters.

The exciting period of GM's 1960s market dominance was told by collector, auto historian, Chevy enthusiast and former Campbell-Ewald catalog copywriter Tony Hossain, while Buick PR veteran, author and journalist Larry Gustin tackled the painful period of the mid-1970s through the 1990s when compliance and survival took precedence over all else. To examine the role of color in design, we turned to the talents of recently retired Chrysler designer and noted auto historian Jeff Godshall. And to tell the tale of how a modern design takes shape, we were joined by GM Global Design chief Ed Welburn. Finally, Ken Gross, well-known auto journalist, historian and former director of the Petersen Automotive Museum, took on the job of documenting the landmarks of GM's modern design resurgence.

Additional contributions came from Art Center College of Design's Transportation Design Department Chair Stewart Reed, who provided design commentary captions, and the Coachbuilt Press Project Manager, Phil Neff, who both found cars and provided extensive historical captions.

We were fortunate to be able to elicit additional editorial contributions from GM Vice Chairman Bob Lutz, who's an avid auto collector, as well as from jewelry designer and dedicated General Motors collector Nicola Bulgari. The final installment came from co-publisher and European car and design authority Richard Adatto, who examined the world-wide migration of design influences.

The words and photos may be the heart of *The Art and Colour of General Motors*, but without the support of Ed Welburn and Teckla Rhoads of GM Design, the GM Archive and GM Heritage Center, it would have been just another book.

Just like great designs such as Chevrolet's original Corvette, a simple idea was the starting point for a diverse team of individuals to do what they do best. I'm hopeful that over the years this finished product will endure as well as that original GM two-seater.

Jonathan Stein is a long-time automotive journalist and historian who has written and edited scores of automotive books and magazine articles and has consulted for museums, auction houses and restorers.

1

All Along the Line:
Inventing General Motors Design

By Phil Patton

The great walls and towers of curing wood marked the frontier. On the edges of the Durant-Dort coachbuilding factory in Flint, Michigan, circa 1900, hardwood was piled in a vast linear castle, awaiting transformation into carriages. In 1908, William Crapo Durant was 47 years old. Working with a partner with the mellifluous name of J. Dallas Dort, Durant had built the company from a seller of two-wheel, $12 carts into the country's largest carriage company, offering a vast array of different models of landaus, phaetons, sulkies and buggies. In the process, Durant created the principle that was to become General Motors' business strategy and ultimately its design strategy—offer a variety of models for different prices and uses. "Playing it safe all along the line," Durant phrased it.

The words were revealing. "Playing," to begin with, reflected Durant's enthusiasm for business. It was not work but fun, and he devoted most of his days and nights to it. But "playing it safe" for Durant denoted something different from the ordinary meaning. The only risks he saw were the risks of missing an opportunity either to buy an enterprise with a bright future or to have a product to offer a customer.

"All along the line" at Durant-Dort meant offering a variety of products. And from carriages, the products eventually became cars.

Flint called itself the "World's Vehicle Capital." The proud, hopeful letters spelling out "Vehicle City" were seen on the rainbow of steel truss across Saginaw Avenue, which was Flint's main drag. The ambiguous word "vehicle" was right: By 1913, the value of automobiles sold surpassed that of carriages.

Billy Durant and the Motorcar

In 1904, the leading citizens of Flint asked Durant to run the infant Buick company founded by plumbing supplier David Dunbar Buick. Under Durant's firm hand, Buick boomed. The company grew so fast that a village of tarpaper and tin shacks, as rambling as the stacks of curing wood, grew up outside Flint to house the hosts of workers who had come to join the enterprise. Buick became the best-selling car in America, and Flint's population of 15,000 quickly expanded.

Durant liked running a car company and believed in the future of the automobile. He set about transferring his ideas from carriages to cars. In a furious year-and-a-half he assembled eleven automobile companies, eight auto parts companies and two commercial vehicle concerns into what became General Motors. Paying for most of the struggling companies with stock, along the way he formulated the "all along the line" philosophy of marketing and design for cars.

The Durant-Dort (misspelled in the original postcard below) coach building factory in Flint, Michigan circa 1900.

Durand-Dort Carriage Company, Flint, Mich.

As Durant explained, "I was for getting every kind of car in sight." His "playing it safe all along the line," was later refined by his successor, Alfred Sloan, into the phrase "a car for every purse and purpose." Later in the century, the idea of a full product line would be emulated by many other industries, from kitchen appliances to radios and cell phones. This design and marketing principle was as important to business as the manufacturing innovations of Eli Whitney or Henry Ford. The sales and design innovations of GM changed business and made design a key part of it. Design was put in the service of sales and the creation of brands.

To understand the idea of "a car for every purse and purpose" more fully, one need simply contrast it with its opposite, embodied in Henry Ford's Model T. Ford did not have a line, he had a model. He called the T the "universal car." Ford's approach could be expressed as a variant of GM's: He offered "ONE car for every purse and purpose."

William Crapo Durant (1861-1947), founded General Motors in 1908 with his philosophy of "playing it safe all along the line."

Ford's strategy was characteristically American and, no-nonsense, plain as the frontier. But Durant was a characteristically American type as well. He was a scrambler, an endlessly energetic man determined not to miss a chance. He would have been right at home in the gold rush days of California.

General Motors turned out to be a pioneer in using design as an instrument for branding, marketing and sales. In this, as in so many areas, the giant company—the first United States corporation to reach a billion dollars in sales—was a model for many others. No wonder it was the object of classic studies by business historians and theorists like Alfred Chandler and Peter Drucker.

The automobile industry circa 1908 was much like the electronics industry in Silicon Valley of more recent times. Promise and enthusiasm were abundant, but it was not clear which technologies would be the most important in the future. "Playing it safe all along the line" for Durant meant buying companies that today are footnotes—Elmore, Cartercar, Marquette, Ewing and Heaney Lamp. Who knew for sure that the Elmore's two-cycle engine was not the way of the future or that the Cartercar's friction drive was a loser, while Buick's valve-in-head engine was a winner?

The truth is that, in 1908 or even 1918, it was far from certain who the winners would be over the long haul. Durant understood this. He did not want to risk not buying the companies that mattered. (He missed out on Ford—Henry Ford wanted $8 million, too much, and in cash—but did grab Cadillac.) William Durant wanted chips down all across the board.

Durant was right to grab up many of the companies. Whether he perceived it or not, things were changing. Automobile historian James Flink records that this was a period of consolidation in the industry. From 253 companies in 1908, when GM was formed, the number fell to just 108 in 1920. It was down to 42 by the end of the 1920s.

Durant's strategy had positioned GM as among the fittest, ready to survive, even as he closed down many of the brands he had acquired. But General Motors suffered financial crises in the turbulent economy of the emerging auto industry. Like the booms and busts of electronic and digital technology of more recent times, the car business grew dramatically, but in fits and starts. Durant himself scrambled, swinging from one financial crisis to another like a trapeze artist escaping by fractions of inches, moving from one restructuring to the next refinancing. His constant mutability and relentless energy for expansion, coupled with lack of focus, exasperated his top lieutenants. Sloan nearly quit GM; Walter Chrysler did. Spreading himself too thin, Durant lost control of GM in 1910, only to regain power in 1915.

The C A R
THAT HAS NO CRANK

Despite the high casualty rate, the auto industry continued to glow brightly for entrepreneurs; about 150 companies entered the market after 1908. No longer was basic utility enough to sell a car. The development of new amenities changed the market: enclosed bodies, better lighting and the self-starter. Introduced by Cadillac in 1912, the self-starter quietly expanded the possibilities for women drivers and enlarged the importance of style and design as selling points. The role of women as buyers grew quickly as the automobile became a symbol of freedom and style, as Virginia Sharf records in *Taking the Wheel: Women and the Coming of the Motor Age* (New York: Free Press, 1991).

The Automobile Matures

General Motors' design began in the early, crude period during which the basic shape of the automobile was being defined. Around 1900, two basic models for what design historians refer to as a "typeform" still battled. The most successful American car of its time, the Curved Dash Oldsmobile of 1901, represented one; it was a "horseless" buggy with the engine under the seat. The curved dash sat in front of the driver and passenger like the front of a snow sleigh. The other arrangement—represented by the 1901 Mercedes, often considered the first fully modern car—put the engine in front of the driver. This configuration had been pioneered by the French Panhard et Levassor in 1891. The système Panhard positioned the engine in front of the driver and used a longitudinal driveshaft to propel the rear wheels. It allowed for a longer, lower car with more flexibility in its packaging. It also introduced the steering wheel in place of the boat-derived tiller.

The first popularly successful American car reflected the roads of the day. Rough country roads required a car with high clearance and tough construction, as seen in the Curved Dash Oldsmobile. European models could count on paved boulevards for much of their traveling, but most American roads were gravel or dirt. Essentially a motorized buggy, at $650 the Curved Dash Olds was the country's first bestseller. Moreover, it attached itself to popular song and jokes, foreshadowing the powerful cultural role of the automobile.

Société Anonyme des Anciens Établissements

PANHARD & LEVASSOR

19, Avenue d'Ivry
PARIS

4. Charrette Anglaise (forme bateau)

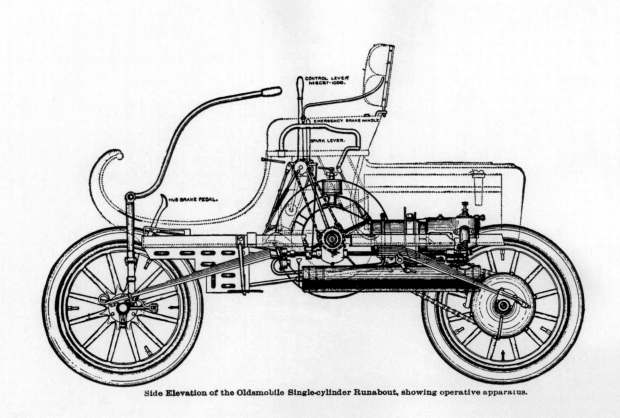

Side **Elevation** of the Oldsmobile **Single-cylinder Runabout,** showing operative apparatus.

Arguably the first step from sheer engineering toward aesthetics in the design of the automobile lay in the smooth fairing of the hood over the engine into the cowl, marking the front of the passenger compartment. But, for the most part, cars of the tens and teens remained loosely joined assemblages of parts. Only a few of them wore elegant bodies echoing coaches of the century before.

That would change, thanks to Durant. As General Motors grew, a new approach evolved to designing this new product. Each of GM's acquisitions had an influence on the others and the common approach. Not necessarily by planning, each company and brand that became part of GM brought something to the whole, some influence and contribution that enlivened the mix and flavored the soup.

Buick was the keystone of GM value in the mix. As Terry B. Dunham and Lawrence Gustin explain in *The Buick: A Complete History*, their definitive history of the brand, Buick was soon established as the bedrock marque for GM. It was the "doctor's car" with high sales, high profits and high reputation. Oldsmobile brought a reputation higher than its sales. It had been the national sales leader until 1905, but by the time Durant bought it, it was in a slump. But soon new models and marketing restored Oldsmobile's fortunes. In 1910 came the Limited, a powerful, attention-getting model advertised in a series of paintings showing it racing an express train. The paintings, by artist William Harden Foster, showed the car blurred with impressionistic streaks suggesting speed. They became nationally famous the way a television ad in a later era might have become.

How much Oldsmobile—and the automobile in general— had advanced in a decade was suggested by a comparison between the Oldsmobile Limited of 1910 and the Curved Dash of ten years earlier. The seven-seat touring car version of the Limited had a six-cylinder, 60 horsepower engine, and massive 42-inch wheels that dwarfed the Curved Dash.

The Standard of the World

Cadillac brought GM the technical standards of creator Henry Leland, who was the master of precision. In style, the brand was conservative. The 1906 Osceola coupe was a piece of coachwork, finely lacquered and pinstriped, and as up-right as a sedan chair in which Dr. Johnson might have been borne across eighteenth century London. Cadillac boasted of "dignity, proportion and richness."

**Cadillac's first closed car, dubbed the "Osceola,"
was built in 1905. For many years, Henry Leland
(shown) used it as personal transportation.
By 1906 this enclosed body style was offered as
a standard model.**

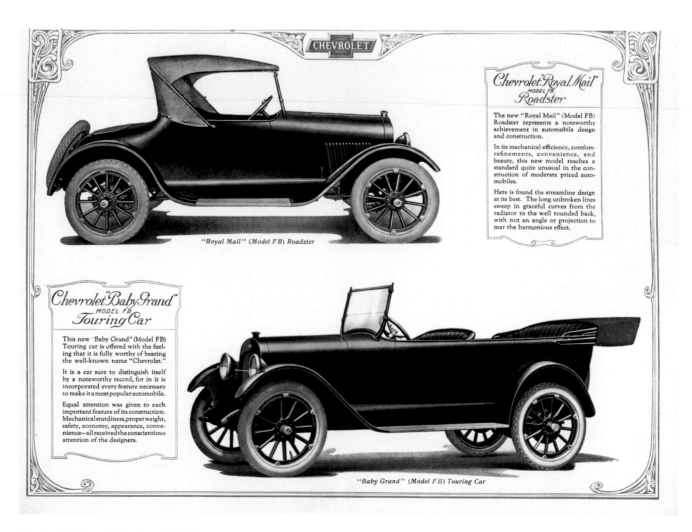

CHEVROLET

Chevrolet "Royal Mail"
MODEL FB
Roadster

The new "Royal Mail" (Model FB) Roadster represents a noteworthy achievement in automobile design and construction.

In its mechanical efficiency, comfort-refinements, convenience, and beauty, this new model reaches a standard quite unusual in the construction of moderate priced automobiles.

Here is found the streamline design at its best. The long unbroken lines sweep in graceful curves from the radiator to the well rounded back, with not an angle or projection to mar the harmonious effect.

"Royal Mail" (Model FB) Roadster

Chevrolet "Baby Grand"
MODEL FB
Touring Car

This new "Baby Grand" (Model FB) Touring car is offered with the feeling that it is fully worthy of bearing the well-known name "Chevrolet."

It is a car sure to distinguish itself by a noteworthy record, for in it is incorporated every feature necessary to make it a most popular automobile.

Equal attention was given to each important feature of its construction. Mechanical sturdiness, proper weight, safety, economy, appearance, convenience—all received the conscientious attention of the designers.

"Baby Grand" (Model FB) Touring Car

The Royal Mail and Baby Grand of 1914 were landmark models for Chevrolet.

Henry Leland had begun his career at the Springfield Armory and had already helped bring interchangeable parts to sewing machines, clocks and adding machines. For automobiles, the parts system was at first more important for building better cars than for building cars better. It was more important for ease of repair than ease of assembly. In 1909, *Scientific American* magazine declared that "standardization and interchangeability of parts will have the effect of giving us a higher grade of motor car at a lower price."

The marque's technical virtues were proven when the company was awarded the Dewar Trophy by the Royal Automobile Club for proving the concept of car-building wholly from interchangeable parts. In 1908, three Model K Cadillacs (red, blue and yellow) were driven 25 miles from London to the Brooklands race track and taken apart. From the resulting shuffle of parts, three new cars were assembled and run. The mixing of parts led to the multicolor effect that resulted in them being dubbed "the harlequin" cars.

Billy Returns with a Vengeance

By 1913, General Motors depended on four brands: Buick, Oldsmobile, Oakland (which evolved into Pontiac) and Cadillac. That all changed in mid-September of 1915, when Billy Durant regained control of General Motors. And when Durant returned, he brought Chevrolet with him. Named after racing driver Louis Chevrolet, this low-price car was the offspring of Durant's own period of years in exile from General Motors.

Design mattered even for GM's newest, most affordable line. The 1914 Chevrolet "Royal Mail" had been pitched as "pleasing to the eye, coming and going." Chevrolet offered proof that Durant searched for a sales advantage and design cues at every level. One tale about the origins of the Chevrolet bowtie logo credits Durant with spotting it in a Sunday newspaper supplement when he was visiting Hol Springs, West Virginia. Another credits his wife, who is said to have plucked it from a wallpaper pattern in a Paris hotel.

As competition for the Model T, however, Chevrolet was still focused on price. The Chevrolet Model 490 of 1915 was designed to be as cheap as the T. Unfortunately, the Chevrolet went on sale not for $490—then the price of the Model T—but for $550. Not for the first time, however, the promise of price was used to catch customer eyes that then lingered to view the cars' style and power. By 1925, the Chevrolet Model K could match the aging T one-for-one in sales.

Another vital acquisition for Durant and GM was not a brand but a man—a visionary executive. In 1916, Alfred Sloan came with the purchase of the Hyatt Roller Bearing Company. With his superb business skills, organization and discipline, Sloan would mold Durant's raw instincts into an irrefutable corporate logic. And when Durant overextended himself and the company in late 1919, Sloan was perfectly placed to lead General Motors into a changing future.

Sloan was Durant refined. Thin and austere of face, he was a bit of a dandy, given to wearing high collars and spats. You might have expected to encounter his lean, sober countenance at a wake—as either the corpse or the undertaker.

In rationalizing Durant's collection of brands into a line, Sloan looked to design and style. Years later, in his classic *My Years With General Motors*, he explained his thinking during that period. From today's perspective, it is easy to forget the basics: The closed car made design and style critical. In the early days of the automobile, cars were open like carriages, not coaches, and they were supplied with folding tops. Driving and riding were outdoor activities.

The arrival of the closed car as a dominant form was critical to Sloan's thinking. Before the mid-1920s, most cars had folding cloth tops. The success of cars such as the inexpensive Essex established the closed car as the norm. The closed car, he wrote, was "by far the biggest single leap" in automobile history since the arrival of the basic car. With the car body now closed—and around 1925 closed cars became the majority of sales—Sloan saw that automobile style would change quickly.

Sloan believed that engineering had reached such a level of maturity that appearance was now the key determinant in sales. So the cut of a fender or hood might influence sales, much like the cut of a skirt or suit would influence sales in the fashion industry. He urged General Motors to look to Europe where such cars as the Hispano-Suiza influenced style as models. Sloan understood that his challenge was to make his cars different from each other and different from year to year.

In particular, Sloan wanted cars to look longer and lower. Just as he had accessorized his suit with spats, he had bought new, smaller wheels to lower his own first car, which

Alfred P. Sloan, Jr. (1875-1966) built General Motors into an international industrial giant and envisioned an essential role for automotive design.

had been a Cadillac. But he wanted also to distinguish car lines by design as well as engine and body size. Durant had crudely taken the same approach, ordering a Buick sliced up and stretched to make a new Oldsmobile. It was brand engineering in its infancy.

For Durant's "all along the line," Sloan supplied the more elegant formulation, "a car for every purse and purpose." Historian Daniel Boorstin famously called this arrangement of brands and models "the ladder of consumption"—from Chevrolet to Oldsmobile to Buick and ultimately to Cadillac. Style would gently nudge buyers up the steps of brands of this ladder. Sometimes, whole new steps had to be created. In 1924-1925, Sloan created the Pontiac line out of Oakland to slip between Chevrolet and Oldsmobile, to fill a gap in price and style.

Sloan gave a new twist to selling and designing all along the line. Fashion houses introduced new lines every year, even every season. In addition to the variety of models offered

Harley Earl's first design for General Motors was
the 1927 LaSalle 303 roadster. Standing behind
Earl, who is behind the wheel, is Cadillac President
Lawrence Fisher, the man responsible for bringing
Earl to Detroit.

in a single year, he wanted to offer a variety of models across years. Sloan admitted he wanted to "create dissatisfaction" with last year's model in order to sell this year's, a phrase later critically paraphrased by others as "manufacturing discontent."

As part of this process, Sloan saw an important role for color. In the era dominated by Ford's black Model T, color was symbolic as well as practical in appeal. It was the most personal and emotional aspect of style and design. And in the marketplace it stood for General Motors' willingness to offer—unlike its competitors—choices to the consumer. To this end, Sloan championed the new fast-drying Duco nitrocellulose lacquers, created by DuPont chemists in 1920. These colors made mass production compatible with color choice. The first use of this approach was on the "True Blue" of Oakland in 1924.

Cars would not have been so bright by the end of the decade had DuPont not taken a stake in General Motors. The investment came thanks to John J. Raskob, the top finance man at the Delaware chemical company, and included the naming of Pierre S. du Pont as president of General Motors. The DuPont company came to value General Motors as a customer for paint and other supplies. In turn, GM was the first automaker to use the innovative Duco fast-drying lacquers.

In effect, General Motors edited Henry Ford's declaration, with his somewhat puritanical defiance of consumers' whims. "Any color you want as long as it's black" became simply "any color you want." The universal car would give way to the personal car.

Sloan needed other ways besides color to introduce excitement into new cars. And, to create that excitement, Sloan looked to Hollywood. There, movie stars and directors drove elaborately customized cars. Many of them were the work of one man, Harley Earl. Earl was brought to Sloan's attention by Lawrence Fisher of Fisher Body, who had moved into management at Cadillac.

Harley Earl had grown up in his family's coachbuilding concern in Los Angeles. Earl Coachworks turned out chariots and wagons for the infant film industry. After attending Stanford, where he was a track star, young Harley moved into designing auto bodies, and his work soon became popular with Hollywood celebrities. Earl styled cars for Tom Mix, Mary Pickford, Cecil B. DeMille and Fatty Arbuckle, the comic actor whose infamous trial fascinated the nation in the 1920s. The Earl company was acquired by Don Lee, the top Cadillac dealer in the Los Angeles area and, thus, Earl did much of his work on Cadillacs.

Fisher and Sloan were impressed with the way Earl conceived each car as a whole—not an assemblage of fenders, hood and other parts—and the way he tested out shapes using modeling clay. With the new methods, Earl could also work fast. In December 1925, they commissioned Earl to style a new line, the LaSalle, which was planned as a less expensive Cadillac. The idea was to offer the first custom style body to a general—if not quite yet mass—market. The result was the 1927 LaSalle.

Soon, Earl would be hired to create the General Motors Art and Colour Section—the forerunner of GM Design. (The British "u," although later dropped, suggested the aspirations to elegance the department represented for Sloan.) In the process, Earl welded Durant and Sloan's "all along the line" to a full line of styles. As the creator of modern auto "styling," he helped express the bond between physical mobility and social and economic mobility laid out in Sloan's ladder of brands. He would tie the automobile irrevocably to the same sort of dreams manufactured by Hollywood. Thanks to Earl, the car biz would become show biz.

Alfred Sloan lived to a ripe old age, laden with honors and in a position to write his own history. The classic, *My Years With General Motors*, laid out his version of how he developed Durant's "all along the line" into the world's largest industrial corporation.

As for Durant, in 1919 he lost control of General Motors for the final time. He later re-entered the automobile industry and also tried his hand at other businesses. The end of the line came when he declared bankruptcy in 1936. He began running a short-order restaurant inside the bowling alley for workers beside the Buick plant in Flint. He died in 1947, but he lived to see the tremendous variety of shapes that emerged from General Motors: the torpedo look and speedlines and fast backs and—as he lay dying—the tailfin was set to surface. Durant had not just experienced but shaped the creation of American automobile design—all along the line.

1903 Cadillac Model A Rear Entry Tonneau

The Model A was truly a carriage without a horse. With no apparent power source, it was probably seen with an element of mystery. – Stewart Reed

1906 Cadillac Model H Coupe

**The 1906 Model H has a small hood up front which suggests
a power unit inside. The upright posture lends a formal and
secure appearance. – SR**

1911 Oldsmobile Limited Touring Car

1914 Chevrolet Baby Grand

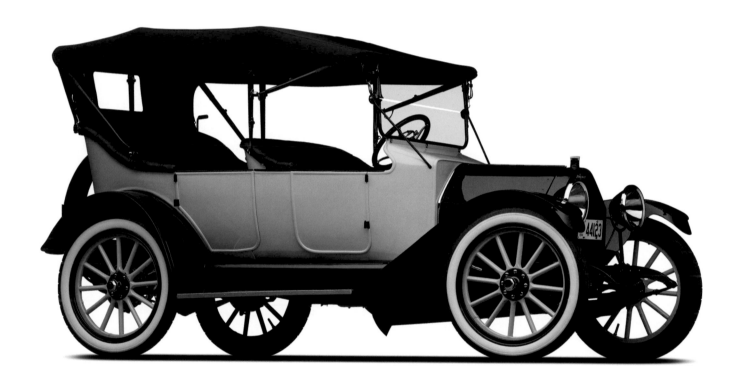

The 1914 Chevrolets had a very light and lively proportion, with notably underslung chassis. The attractive and lithe styling was intended to help the better equipped Chevrolets in their sales battle with the less expensive Ford Model T.
– SR

1914 Chevrolet Royal Mail

1914 Chevrolet Royal Mail

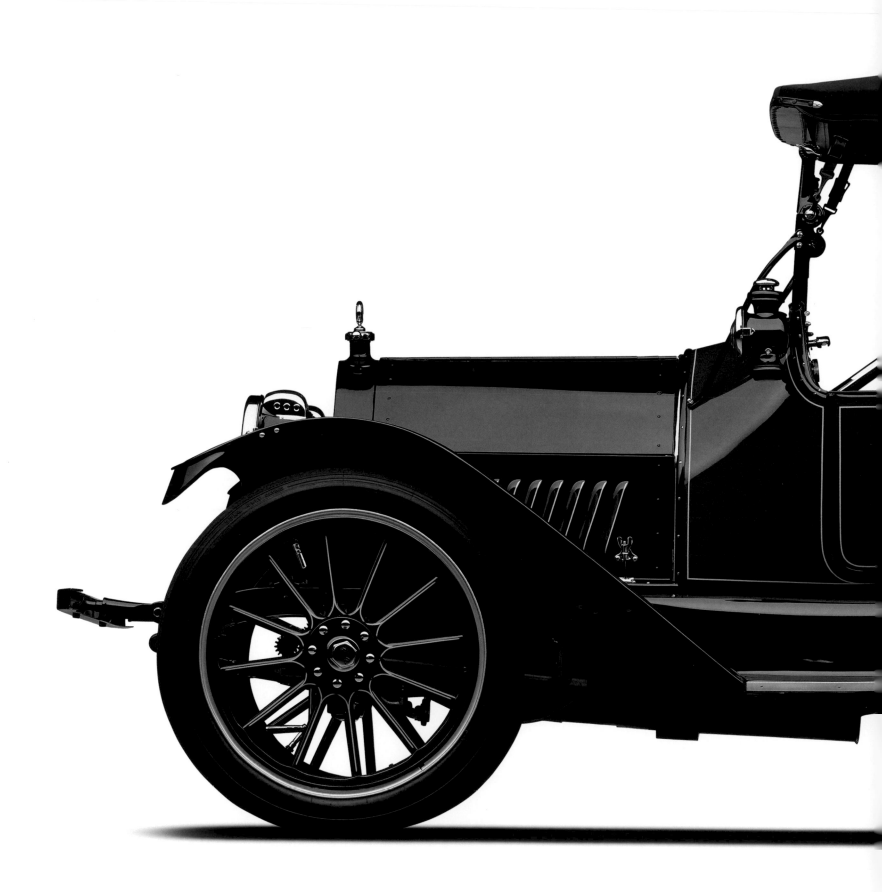

1920 Cadillac Type 59 Limousine by Don Lee

No longer a carriage with a top, but a fully enclosed form,
this one-off Harley Earl-designed Cadillac Type 59 bodied by
Don Lee Coachworks featured smooth surface transitions
and a two-tone paint scheme. With color up to the roof, it
emphasizes visual length and draws attention to the secure,
closed cabin. – SR

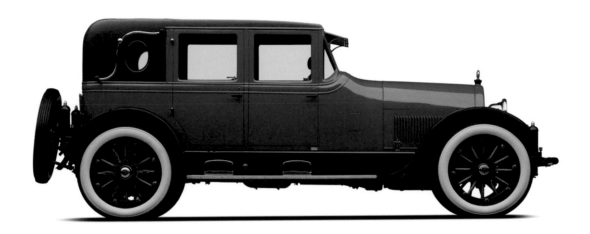

1927 LaSalle 303 Roadster

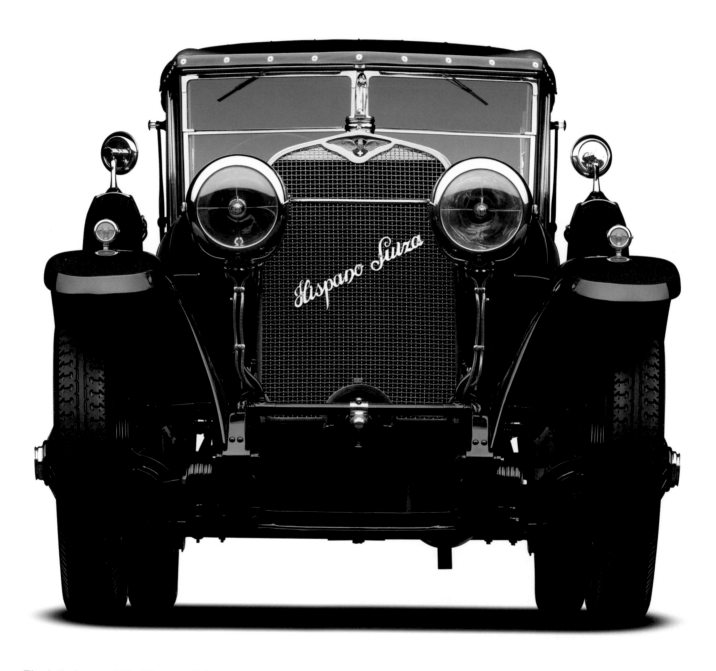

The tall stance of the Hispano-Suiza H6B gives it an imposing and powerful look. It is contrasted here with the 1927 LaSalle, which presents a somewhat lower, more stable emphasis with lower headlamps centered on the fender tops and a twin band bumper. This was the first American production car to have a coachbuilder's level of design sophistication and detail. – SR

1927 LaSalle 303 Roadster

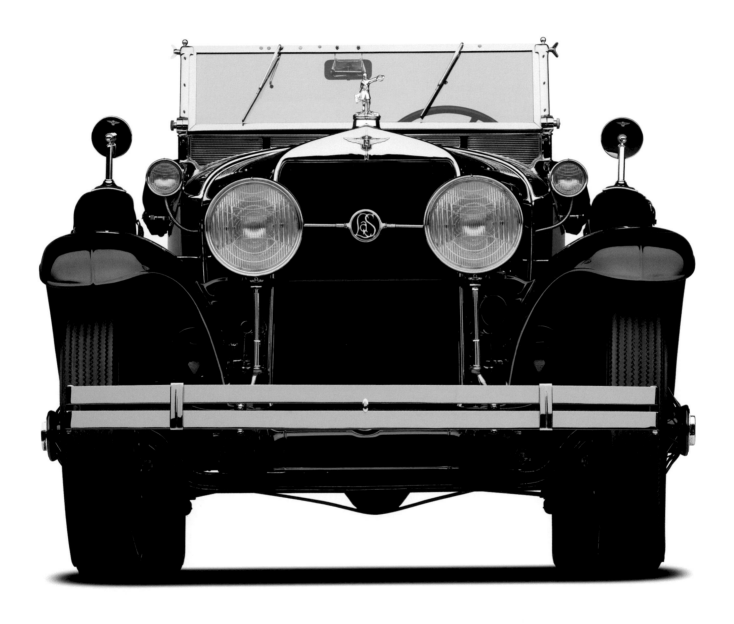

1923 Hispano-Suiza H6B, 1927 LaSalle 303 Roadster

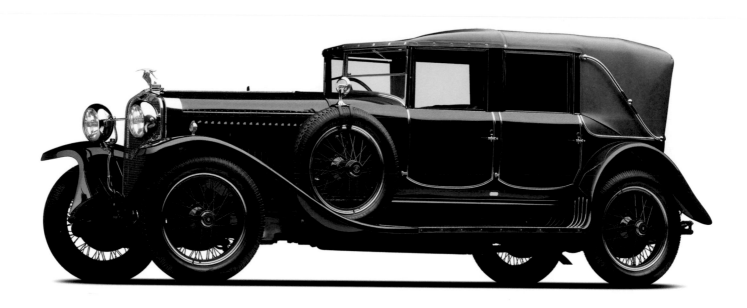

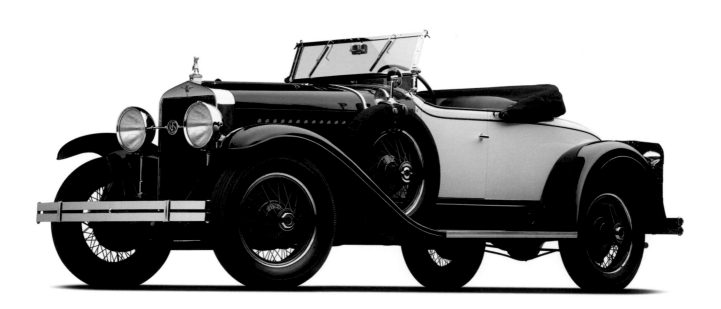

2

Styling Legitimized:
Harley Earl Comes to Town

By Terry V. Boyce

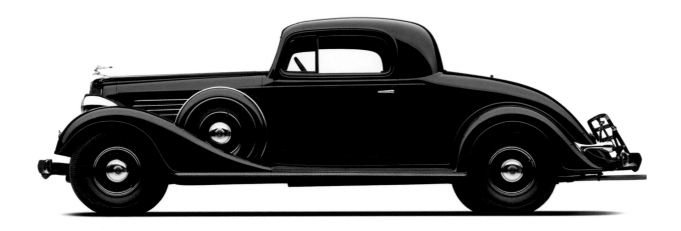

In June 1927, the General Motors Art and Colour Section opened for business with Harley J. Earl at the helm. GM thus became the first automaker of consequence to dedicate corporate staff to automobile styling. Sorting out the business of designing cars on a grand scale would take more than a decade. During that time, Harley Earl would implement the annual model change, introduce car-body sharing across multiple divisions, and master the art of communicating automotive value and prestige through appearance. In the midst of it all, he would establish General Motors as the style leader of the American automobile industry. Alfred P. Sloan, Jr. was the corporate genius who made a Harley Earl possible. Even before becoming president of GM in 1923, Sloan had envisioned a central activity dedicated to styling the multitude of vehicles produced by GM divisions.

In 1926, the Fisher Body Company, partially owned by GM since 1919, was fully absorbed into General Motors. Fisher built virtually all of the corporation's closed car bodies, accounting for about 75 percent of General Motors' production. Sloan saw the creation of the new Fisher Body operating division as an opportunity to deal with several issues related to automotive styling.

A reasonable level of automotive reliability and performance had become a given by the mid-1920s. With the automobile's functionality ensured, Sloan could see that appearance was becoming ever more important to buyers. Sloan was well aware of the impact of the "color revolution," not only on cars but also on consumer products in general. He also appreciated the growing influence of women on purchasing decisions.

Art and Colour Comes to Life

On June 23, 1927, Sloan obtained approval from the General Motors Executive Committee to establish a "special department" within General Motors ". . . to study the question of art and color combinations in General Motors products." The job description for the department head suggested a broader role: the new manager would "direct production body design" and "conduct research and development programs in special car design." Sloan named the new group "The Art and Colour Section."

The ideal candidate to run Art and Colour had, almost magically, already appeared. He was, of course, 33-year-old Harley Earl, who had come east in 1926 to design the 1927 LaSalle for Cadillac's Larry Fisher. Sloan would later write of the original LaSalle, "It was the first stylist's car to achieve success in mass production."

Earl's talents and design philosophies were remarkably well suited to Sloan's vision of a central styling staff. The GM president considered the tall, narrow sedans of the mid-1920s unattractive. He also believed that their high center of gravity could make them unsafe. Earl was already making cars longer and lower in appearance, if not in fact. His portfolio of California custom creations provided ample evidence of his talents in this aspect of design.

Harmony in Design

Earl was also in sync with Sloan's desire to achieve more unity in vehicle appearance. The GM president had noted a major disconnect in the very way cars were designed. Chassis engineers designed not only the chassis, but also all parts bolted to it—including the fenders, radiator shell and even lamps. Meanwhile, the wood-framed metal body was typically designed, built, painted and trimmed by a specialist supplier. "The final appearance of the cars reflected the independence of the two operations," Sloan would dourly recall.

Many of the full custom cars Earl had built for his Hollywood clients were styled so that all visible components harmonized with the overall design. His sensational 1927 LaSalle would prove the success of this approach for a production car.

On the practical side, the young Californian was using advanced techniques to style cars. To finesse and proof designs, he adopted the little-known technique of creating three-dimensional models in clay.

Then there was Earl's towering physique and authoritative personality. Sloan bet that the brashly confident, yet affably charming, Earl could convince GM's virtually autonomous divisional leaders to accept input from a central corporate design group.

There was one more consideration: By 1927, Sloan had already conceived an annual model change policy for GM. The goal was to make GM cars visually fresh every year, enhancing their appeal and keeping them fashionable, even if technical advances were minimal. Sloan knew the daunting task of orchestrating the annual model change across the broad GM product line would require a leader with more than extraordinary talents and vision.

According to the book by Michael Lamm and Dave Holls, *A Century of Automotive Style*, Sloan was especially taken with Earl's obvious drive "to be first in everything, particularly in fashion." Earl was committed to leading American automotive styling—and would remain so throughout much of his career at GM.

Sloan promised Earl that, at least initially, the chain of command would link directly to his office. (Earl would continue to hold, but rarely wield, the all-powerful Sloan card for decades to come, while making no secret of the fact he held it.) A staff of 50, including 10 stylists, was originally budgeted for Art and Colour. An in-house headhunter was quickly appointed to find and screen applicants.

In his first months at Art and Colour, Earl surely worked with GM "corporate colorist" H. Ledyard Towle to finalize the designs and establish the multitude of "Nature's Studios" color options for the 1928 Cadillacs. (Towle, a fine artist, was on loan from DuPont, where he had advised the paint company's clients on color trends since the mid-1920s.) Earl also began developing models for the forthcoming 1930 Cadillac V-16. Chevrolet's Ormond L. Hunt became Earl's first non-Cadillac "customer" when he stopped by to request help with his division's 1928 models.

COLOR CREATIONS FROM

Nature's Studios

REVEALING HER MASTERLY MANIPULATION

OF COLOR THROUGH THE MEDIUM OF

SUPERB MOTOR CAR CREATIONS

FISHER BODY CORPORATION

FLEETWOOD BODY CORPORATION

GENERAL MOTORS

The important 1928 color option brochure, *Color Creations from Nature's Studios,* was created by "corporate colorist" H. Ledyard Towle and Harley Earl.

A group of General Motor's executives including Alfred Sloan (center), Harley Earl (far right) and the Fisher brothers.

Earl staffed his new department with talent from the many recently defunct classic custom coachbuilders. They pioneered many design techniques still employed today, such as clay modeling (above left), full-scale drawings and color rendering (above right).

The first completely new car from Art and Colour would be the 1929 Buick—and it would be remembered as a disaster! Working with some of his first stylists, Earl designed a Buick sedan with a new, lower roofline and arched side windows. The body rolled out slightly in cross-section, just below the beltline, to accent the car's lowness. This made the light reflect off the curvature of the painted metal and created a horizontal highlight below the windows, accenting the car's low roofline.

Earl always maintained he was happy with the 1929 Buick as released to production engineers. But when he saw the actual car, he "roared like a Ventura sea lion." The roofline had been raised and the design so otherwise altered that it was no longer the car he'd envisioned. The body "bulge" remained, but it now seemed awkward.

Supposedly it was Walter P. Chrysler who first dubbed it "the Pregnant Buick." Newspapers picked up the derisive nickname and Buick sales slowed. Earl would remember the 1929 Buick as a painful lesson well learned. Henceforth, he would insist on final approval of vehicles after production engineering changes were made.

During his first years at GM, Harley Earl was greatly involved in the battle to maintain and enhance Cadillac prestige in a luxury car world market then crowded with both new and long-established contenders. Although Fisher was responsible for the bodies of cataloged Cadillac models, most of the custom bodies for GM's top nameplate came from the Fleetwood Metal Body Company, a highly respected Pennsylvania coachbuilder that Fisher had acquired in 1925. After Fisher officially closed the Fleetwood plant during January 1931, operations were moved from Pennsylvania to Detroit.

Among the first cars completed in the new Fleetwood Detroit plant were the Harley Earl-designed Madame X Cadillac V-16s. (Earl personally provided the name, too, borrowing it from a popular play of the day.) The slanted windshield, thin roof pillars and other special body features that characterized the Madame X V-16s made them some of the most coveted sedans on the road.

Common Bodies

By the time the V-16 Cadillac went into production, the nation was already sliding into the financial maelstrom of the Great Depression. At a time when every cost-control measure counted, Earl initiated and helped implement a body-sharing program that saved General Motors millions. The idea originated with Vincent D. Kaptur, Sr., supervisor of body development for Art and Colour. As Kaptur reviewed Fisher Body drawings for the various divisions, he noted that the dimensions of many parts and stampings were nearly identical—differences were so minute as to be imperceptible to customers. Why not make parts common when possible and share them across divisions? The savings in engineering and tooling costs would be enormous.

Earl took Kaptur's findings to GM management, and it became a policy to share body structures and hardware whenever possible. By 1933, several Fisher body shells were shared by the divisions; the savings helped keep Buick, Oldsmobile, and Pontiac afloat financially. Soon, almost all GM cars were based on one of four basic body designs. Internally they were designated, from smallest to largest, Fisher A-, B-, C-, and D-bodies.

Visually orchestrating Alfred Sloan's "a car for every purse and purpose" price ladder was a major challenge for Earl. The 1931 GM offerings, for example, were organized into a tidy menu that started with the $475 Chevrolet Roadster and extended all the way up to the $9,700 Cadillac V-16 Town Brougham. In between were dozens of models offered under five additional nameplates. Earl had to provide the visual and tactile styling cues that supported the price ladder. Each year's new Oldsmobile needed to be slightly less desirable in appearance and trim than a Buick, but obviously more desirable and somewhat more richly appointed than a Pontiac, and so forth.

Harley Earl's particular genius was that he could ably and consistently signify the relative value of GM cars through the nuances of wheelbase, moldings, bright trim and accoutrements. It helped that he was a collector of design ideas. Some were garnered from annual trips to Europe's coachbuilder salons, where the latest styles in automotive fashion were exhibited. Others sprang from aircraft, boat and architectural design. But most ideas came from the drawing boards of his stylists. If a sketch for a hubcap, fender lamp or ornament caught Earl's eye but had no immediate application, it would be filed away for renewed consideration later.

Perhaps Earl's most difficult challenge as head of Art and Colour was managing an ever-changing, ever-growing staff of stylists employed, first and foremost, for their artistic talents. Some stayed but a short while, unable or unwilling to adapt to the Art and Colour culture, which required passionate dedication in an atmosphere of what has been called "anonymous creativity." Others would find a satisfying career in the GM studios. Many would spend decades, often working literally day and night, under the direction of the sometimes imperious, often brusque, yet disarmingly charismatic, "Mister Earl."

In the midst of the Depression, automotive design came to a fork in the road. Deciding the direction GM would take would be of enormous importance to its future success—and it was largely dependent upon Harley Earl's call.

The limited production 1930-31 Madame X Cadillac V-16 was an early example of Art and Colour's work. The Madame X design was characterized by a slanted windshield and thin roof pillars.

Art and Colour stylists work on the clay model for the 1933 Cadillac Aerodynamic Coupe, which is considered GM's first purpose-built show car. It was displayed in the GM pavilion at the 1933-34 "Century of Progress" Chicago World's Fair.

Popular Streamlining

Revolutionary aerodynamic designs based on wind tunnel studies, which originated with Europeans such as Paul Jaray, pointed to one path. By 1932, numerous proposals for scientifically aerodynamic cars, often mid- or rear-engined, regularly appeared in technical journals and mainstream publications. Many resembled stub-nosed teardrops; others were distinctly insect-like.

An alternate path, based more on aesthetics than science, led to evolutionary designs. The 1932 Graham Blue Streak, designed by Murray Body chief designer Amos Northup, set the standard for popular streamlining. Overnight, it made every other production car obsolete. With its slanted and V-shaped radiator grille, valanced fenders, slanted (and visor-less) windshield and low roofline, the new Graham appeared to "cut" through the air like a ship through water. Minimal bright work and a monochromatic paint treatment helped unify its design.

Aerodynamic purists huffed that cars such as the Graham were only seven percent more efficient in the wind tunnel than a boxy 1925 sedan, while scientifically streamlined concepts proved up to 35 percent more efficient. Popular streamlining proponents countered that pure aerodynamics made little difference in the real-world operation of the era's automobiles, where speeds rarely exceeded 50 mph.

During 1933, the GM Customer Research Staff was formed to serve as a "Proving Ground of Customer Opinion." Surveys soon put the question of scientific streamlining vs. popular streamlining before the public. Results showed that car buyers preferred the flowing speed lines of popular streamlining to aerodynamically superior shapes—by a wide margin.

Harley Earl liked to know what car buyers were thinking. The Customer Research surveys would provide him with many useful insights as he sought to advance automotive design without crossing what Customer Research called "the boundary line of public acceptance."

However, the 1933 GM cars had already adopted the attributes of popular streamlining. The Cadillac V-16 Aerodynamic Coupe, shown by GM at the 1933 Chicago World's Fair, blended a streamlined fastback body with the contemporary styling of the 1933 V-16. This combination provided a restrained but exceedingly handsome glimpse of the styling direction GM would subsequently take. (A run of 20 production Aerodynamic Coupes would follow, built during 1934-1937.)

It was left to the Chrysler Corp., ruled at the time by engineers, to roll out America's first scientifically streamlined production cars—the 1934 Chrysler and DeSoto Airflows. Even with their impressive structural strength, roomy interiors and ultra-modern appearance, they were unsuccessful. The Airflow had gone too far, too fast.

The triumph of popular streamlining helped make annual updates and revisions possible. Valanced fenders, shrouded radiator grilles and covered fuel tanks gave designers more exterior sheet metal to sculpt and vary as design evolved to the measured cadence of the annual model change. It would be much more difficult to restyle a teardrop each year.

By 1934, Harley Earl had a new LaSalle in his pocket that could take popular streamlining to the next level. Getting it into production, though, turned out to be a cliffhanger.

During 1931-1933, the LaSalle had become a near-Cadillac in both price and appearance. Sales lagged and GM management planned to cancel the nameplate after 1933. About then, Harley Earl spotted a set of drawings by Fleetwood stylist Jules Agramonte that depicted a car with a tall, narrow grille (inspired by English beach racers of the time), "pontoon" fenders and a clean, lithe form. Earl saw in the drawings a new LaSalle that could rival the impact of the 1927 original.

However, when GM executives met to view the proposed 1934 GM line, there was no LaSalle among the styling models. Just as the meeting was concluding, Earl stepped forward. "Gentlemen," he said, "if you decide to discontinue the LaSalle, this is the car you are not going to build . . ." As he spoke, curtains parted to reveal a striking sedan developed from Agramonte's sketches. The executives were mesmerized. Within minutes, the 1934 LaSalle was approved for production.

The 1934 LaSalle was a pioneering example of the art moderne style that would characterize not only cars but also every sort of consumer product in the second half of the 1930s. The LaSalle contributed enormously to making GM the automotive style leader—and it added greatly to the stature Earl and his Art and Colour Section held within the corporation.

An innovative feature of the 1934 LaSalle was its standard enclosed spare tire. The introduction of an independent front suspension made the enclosed spare practical. It allowed the engine to be placed over the front suspension—which meant the seating package could also shift forward, permitting a trunk large enough to accommodate both luggage and the spare. By 1936, many GM sedans would feature a squared deck lid that further increased trunk space.

Having saved the LaSalle, Harley Earl took on a much greater challenge—rescuing Buick. Once the crown jewel of the GM brands, Buick, victimized by a staid product line and collapsing sales, had fallen on very hard times. A young and dynamic GM comer named Harlow H. "Red" Curtice took on management of the nearly moribund division in late 1933.

A salesman shows off the "Turret Top" on a new General Motors car. GM pioneered this industry-leading roofline in 1935 on most of their closed models.

The official pace car of the 1934 Indianapolis 500 was this 1934 LaSalle 350 convertible coupe. It was driven by Willard "Big Boy" Rader, who also had been tapped to drive the '27 LaSalle and '31 Cadillac V-16 at previous Memorial Day classics.

After meeting with Earl to review proposals for future Buicks, Curtice challenged the styling chief to come back with a Buick that Earl would like to drive himself. The result would be the stylish 1936 Buicks. Their poised and powerful look was supported by new engines offering extraordinary performance. Launched with a sophisticated ad campaign that perfectly matched the tone of the times, the 1936 Buicks found quick acceptance in a year that saw the nation's economic recovery strengthen. Buick's dramatic turnaround helped make 1936 GM's best sales year since 1929.

Progress in manufacturing and engineering enabled several important styling advances in the mid-1930s. After steel mills developed the capability to produce single sheets of steel wide enough to form a car roof, GM introduced industry-leading steel Turret Tops on most 1935 closed models. The Turret Top eliminated the complex composite wood-frame roof insert, a particular bane of earlier closed car owners. The hypoid rear axle was an engineering innovation that made it possible to lower the drive shaft, permitting a lower passenger floor and overall body height. Drop-center frame designs allowed body engineers to lower passenger floors and seating, allowing for a lower roofline.

Art and Colour was coming up with its own innovations, too. The 1935 Pontiac featured a wide, ribbed bright streak running along the center of the hood and down the grille. This "Silver Streak" was adapted from stylist Franklin Q. Hershey's 1933 Art and Colour design contest entry. It became a Pontiac trademark, used through 1956, and it was a pioneering example of how a styling device can help brand a product.

On December 6, 1935, Harley Earl hired 23-year-old William L. Mitchell, an artist and car enthusiast whose portfolio of boldly imaginative automotive illustrations greatly impressed the GM styling chief. Mitchell was immediately put to work on a LaSalle sedan concept. Initiated as a response to the 810 Cord, the car evolved into the trendsetting 1938 Cadillac Sixty Special sedan. Within a year, Mitchell became head of the Cadillac studio and would eventually succeed Harley Earl as GM styling chief upon Earl's retirement in late 1958.

During 1936, Earl began to rotate some Art and Colour designers to Europe for a stint at Opel, which had been controlled by GM since 1929. The German design studio became something of an advance design and body engineering center. As early as 1936, Opel offered a unit-bodied Olympia small car. Senior Kapitan models for 1938 featured an extended front fender line that would be first seen stateside on the 1941 Cadillac Sixty Special.

In the United States, new Fisher A- and B-bodies for 1937 were all-steel in construction. GM cars of that year, and their mildly face-lifted 1938 counterparts, were very popular. For 1937, Buick sales alone were more than four times those of 1933.

A Rose by Any Other Name

Harley Earl and his stylists had a milestone year in 1937, when they moved into larger and more prominent quarters occupying eight floors of a building just behind GM headquarters. At the same time, Alfred Sloan changed the name of Art and Color (the "u" had already been dropped from "colour") to the GM Styling Section. This pleased Earl, who

Top - In early 1938, dealers sent out Western Union telegrams inviting potential buyers to test-drive the all new Cadillac Sixty Special. The new model helped boost Cadillac's fortunes with an astounding 254 percent sales increase.

Middle - The 1938 Buick Y-Job was Harley Earl's first concept car. Built by General Motors Styling (as the Art and Colour Section had become) on a Buick chassis, for Earl's personal use. It was first displayed in public at Mr. Sloan's Industrial Luncheon at the Waldorf=Astoria in 1940.

Bottom - This Pontiac publicity shot illustrates the 1935 Silver Streak with its characteristic wide ribbed bright trim running along the center of the hood and down the grille. Variations of this styling theme appeared on Pontiacs well into the 1950s.

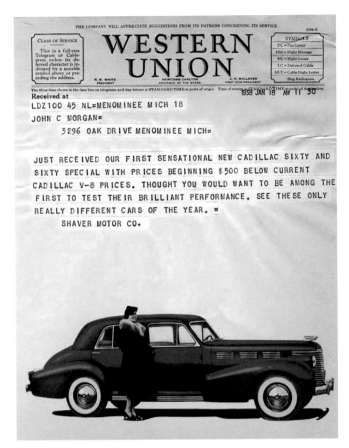

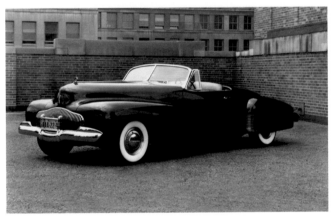

had never liked the original designation. It was a good year for Sloan, too; he became GM Chairman of the Board during 1937.

The expanded real estate allowed Earl to create separate and locked studios for each division. As the only executive holding a master set of keys, he could better control design development across the studios. Earl also started an advanced design studio to explore future automotive forms, while the rest of his organization continued to focus on models two years ahead.

As the Styling Section expanded, Earl brought a number of fresh and highly talented young designers into the GM Styling studios. At the time of Earl's passing in 1969, the vice presidents of styling for all four of America's largest automakers would be men who had started their careers at GM Styling: Bill Mitchell at GM, Gene Bordinat at Ford, Elwood Engel at Chrysler and Dick Teague at American Motors.

In January 1938, the Cadillac Sixty Special made its debut at the New York Auto Show. It would influence sedan styling in general for more than a decade. Its lack of running boards would spur the entire industry to give them up.

During 1938, Harley Earl designed a one-off car for his personal use. He named it "the Y-Job" ("Y" being the military code designation for prototype aircraft at the time). Built on a Buick chassis, it was completed during 1939. The sleek Y-Job predicted many styling trends, especially for forthcoming Buicks. Earl drove the Y-Job daily for many years and considered it his "laboratory on wheels." Today, Earl's Y-Job is proudly maintained at the General Motors Heritage Center, rightfully treasured as the original GM concept car.

Most 1939 GM production cars featured new Fisher bodies with larger window openings that allowed for greater visibility. That year's Buick featured a wide, low grille inspired by European Grand Prix cars of the era. The new Cadillacs had a sharply pointed prow—which was emulated by the 1939 Chevrolets to the delight of owners who enjoyed owning a "baby Cadillac." Both Oldsmobile and Pontiac offered new value-price models utilizing the Chevrolet A-body.

The extremely popular 1940 models would propel GM to a record sales year. Especially in demand were sedan models using the new Fisher C-body—their rooflines and rounded decks were obviously inspired by the Cadillac Sixty Special. Every division but Chevrolet offered versions. More than 1.6 million new GM cars would be registered during 1940, a record 47.6 percent of the U.S. market. (In 1926, GM market share had been only 27.6 percent).

During 1940, publicity photos of Harley Earl and his Y-Job were distributed to newspapers and magazines. Already legendary within the close-knit world of automotive designers, Earl had heretofore been largely unknown to the public. But that was about to change.

On September 3, 1940, Harley Earl was named a General Motors vice president, the first stylist ever appointed to such a position in the auto industry. His Styling Section had grown to include more than 300 talented stylists, clay modelers, and metalworkers. In addition to the cars and trucks produced by GM, Styling also designed the locomotives, kitchen appliances, storage batteries and other products manufactured by the many General Motors Divisions.

Within a few weeks of Earl's promotion, GM dealer showrooms would be crowded with customers coming in to view the new 1941 models. Cadillac, Buick, Oldsmobile and Pontiac would reveal attractive fastback styles based on a new Fisher B-body. Freshened versions of popular notchback styles would also be shown, many finished in popular two-tone paint combinations.

Across the board, the 1941 offerings were the most visually pleasing and richly detailed GM cars yet. Heavily chromed 1941 Buicks fairly sparkled with the synergy of the enduring Harlow Curtice/Harley Earl relationship. The new, boldly styled Cadillac line for 1941 would become a runaway sales success, helped by the new, lower priced Cadillac Series 61, which replaced the discontinued LaSalle. And the all-important Chevrolets, whose volume and profits were at the core of GM's success, were longer, larger and better equipped than any previous models.

As the 1941 cars were being introduced, the GM Styling staff was finishing their 1942 designs. New premium-line fastback coupes and enhanced notchback sedans for 1942 would be the most modern cars on the road. Of course, the 1942 cars would be produced only briefly, as Pearl Harbor triggered the total conversion of the auto industry to the production of war materiel. But the '42s would return, with styling revisions, after World War II; some derivative styles would be offered through 1948.

On the same 1940 September day that the GM Executive Board approved Earl's promotion, it also accepted the resignation of GM President William S. Knudsen. At President Roosevelt's request, Knudsen was on his way to Washington to run the nation's raidly expanding war production program.

Even with war clouds gathering on the horizon, Harley Earl, the 46-year-old newly appointed Vice President of Styling for the world's largest automaker, was no doubt looking forward, with more confidence than ever, to a future he would help shape.

Opposite - In January of 1936, 23-year-old Bill Mitchell was assigned by Harley Earl to design a new Cadillac model. His first complete design was the Series Sixty Special, which he presented in this rendering.

1928 Chevrolet National Model AB Two-Door Coach

Chevrolet's 1928 National Coach displays a very tidy,
organized design, with a continuously painted surface
that stops at the top and emphasizes the closed body.
Equally well-organized details include a design line below
the belt and body-color disc wheels with contrasting
demountable wheel rims. - Stewart Reed

1932 Chevrolet Confederate Cabriolet

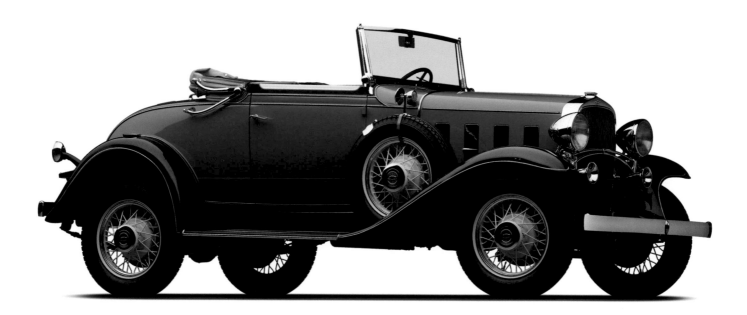

GM's moderately priced models show many of the cues from
the company's more flamboyant and expensive senior lines.
From the jaunty, compact Chevrolet to the slightly longer
hood and proportional differences of the Oakland and
Marquette, these cars each have distinctive personalities.
- SR

1930 Marquette Roadster, 1931 Oakland Cabriolet,
1932 Chevrolet Confederate Cabriolet

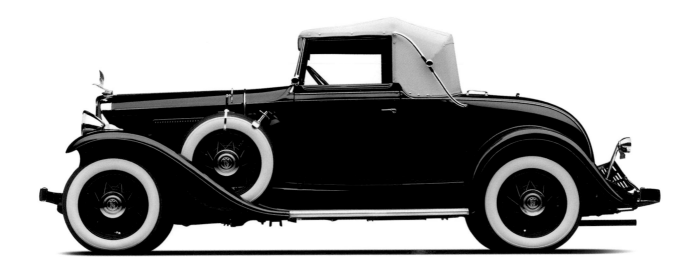

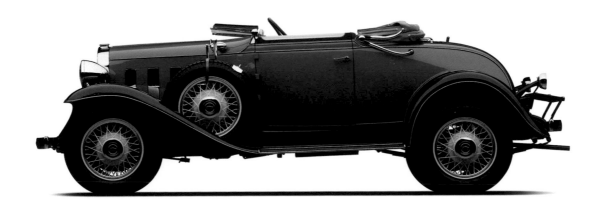

1935 Buick 96S Coupe

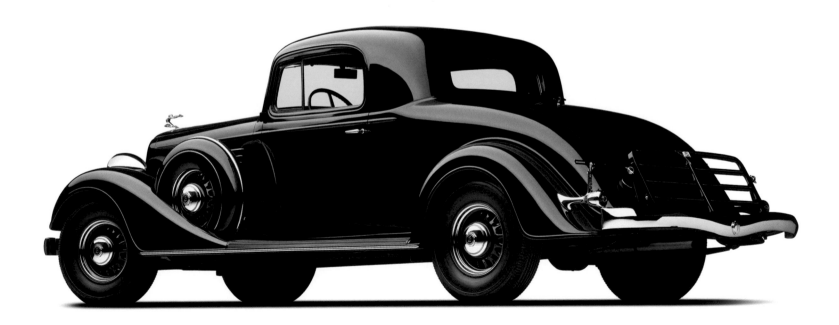

1934 LaSalle Series 350 Convertible Coupe

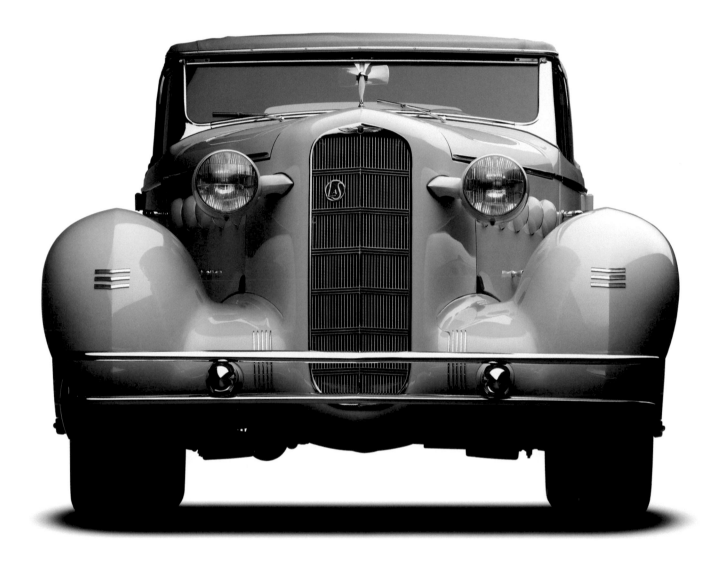

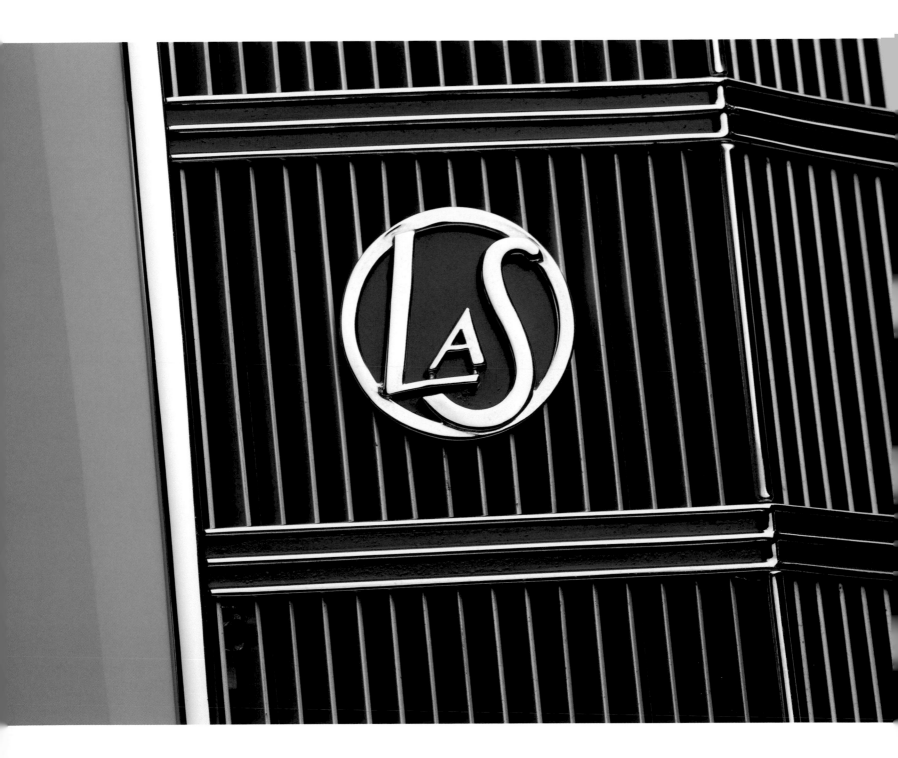

1934 LaSalle Series 350 Convertible Coupe

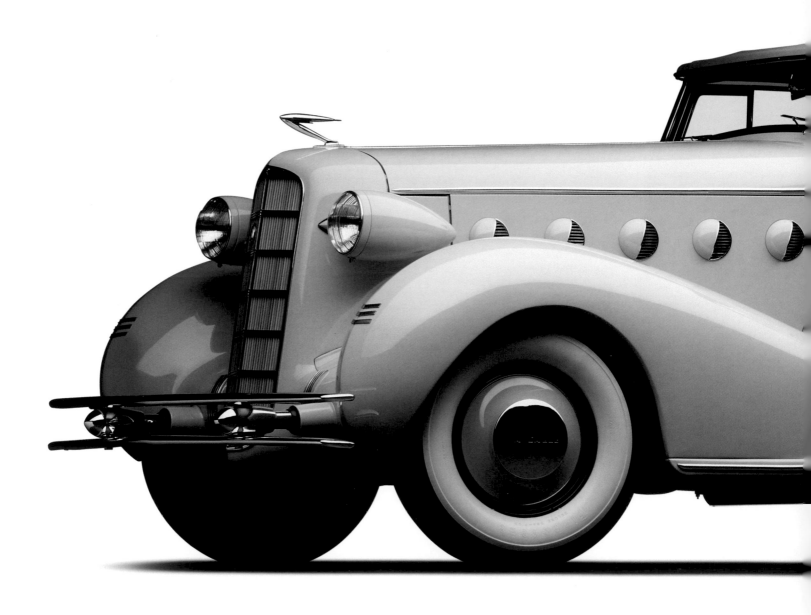

This beautiful convertible coupe is a remarkably international design. It is dramatic in proportion, yet smooth and understated in its fine details. The peaked fender shapes (as evidenced on page 62) repeat beautifully front to rear. – SR

1931 Cadillac V-16 Series 452B Dual Cowl Phaeton

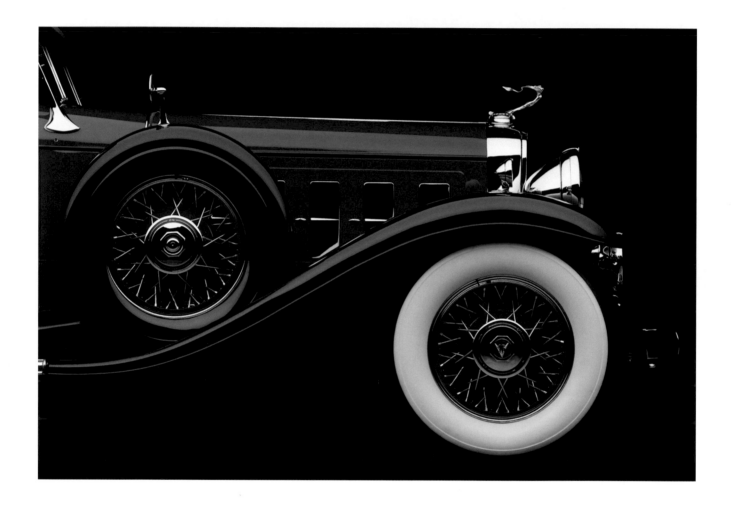

1931 Cadillac V-16 Series 452B Dual Cowl Phaeton

1937 Cadillac V-16 Series 90 Aerodynamic Coupe

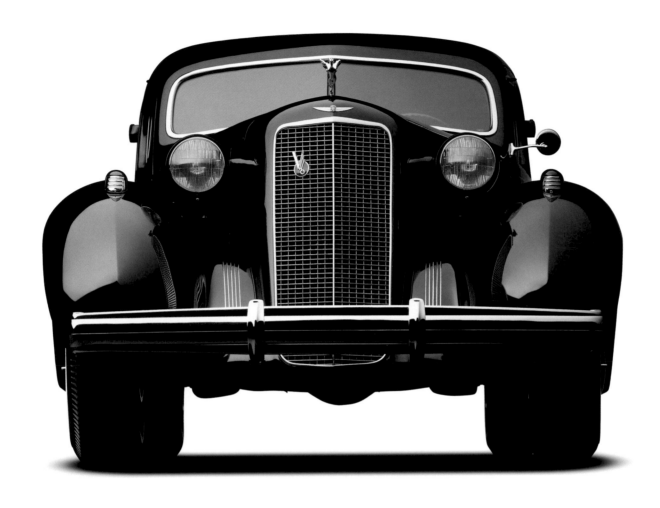

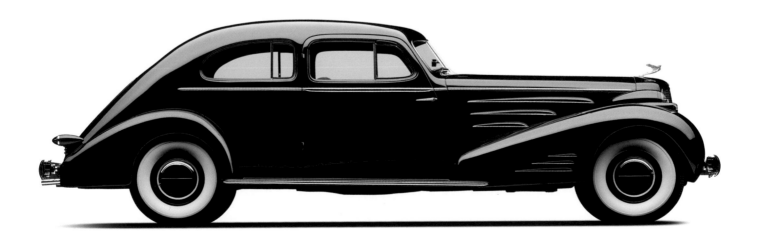

1938 Cadillac Sixty Special

Cadillac's Sixty Special is a very disciplined, smooth and integrated design, which is completely in step with the art deco fashion and architecture of the era. Details such as window trim, lamps and grille are beautifully understated and refined. - SR

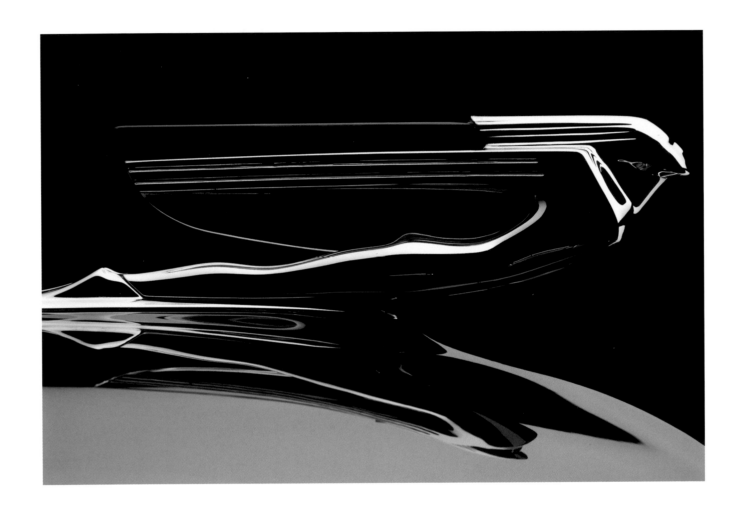

1938 Buick Y-Job

A concept car, the Buick Y-Job was the first of many successful design advances to gauge public response and to strongly develop brand consciousness. This profoundly important design was one of the first to emphasize a bold, wide, horizontal front theme vs. a vertical theme. Notice the smooth hidden head-lamp covers. - SR

1939 Buick Special Series 40 Convertible Sedan

1940 Oldsmobile Series 90 Sedan

3

General Motors Goes Showbiz: GM's Great Traveling Displays Hit the Road

By Michael Lamm

Part circus, part road show, part Broadway, GM's two major traveling exhibits, the Caravan/Parade of Progress and the Motorama extravaganzas, mixed education with pure entertainment. Admission was always free, and both types of shows became instant hits. Millions of Americans flocked to see them year after year, and no one ever walked away disappointed. General Motors launched the first Caravan of Progress in 1936, changing the name to Parade of Progress in 1941. The GM Transportation Unlimited/Motorama series followed in 1949 and for a while, both types of shows ran simultaneously. The earlier Caravan/Parade played mostly to audiences in smaller towns and cities, while Motoramas were shown in large metropolitan areas such as New York, Boston, Chicago, Miami, San Francisco and Los Angeles.

The Streamliners stood on 232-inch GMC truck chassis and used conventional gasoline engines. Six Streamliners, parked three to a side with a broad canvas awning stretched overhead between them, formed the Caravan's midway. The seventh Streamliner usually stood under a 1200-seat tent at the far end of the midway. In the first Caravan, this seventh Streamliner contained a stage that opened out for lectures and demonstrations. The eighth Streamliner became a spare in case one of the others broke down.

According to Ed Bracken, who joined the Caravan in 1936 and later became GM's corporate projects manager, the show's staff of "Caravaneers" consisted of 40-50 men in their early 20s, all single, all college graduates, many from Ivy League schools. "It was our job," he recalled, "to drive the trucks and, on arrival at the site, change into coveralls and set up the show. After that, we put on suits, ties and white caps and became lecturers on the exhibits. At the end of each two-to-four-day visit, we'd pack up and drive to the next town."

Everyone hired on as a lecturer, but there was an apprenticeship period when each man learned every job. Duties included cleaning up the grounds, washing the vehicles, setting up and tearing down exhibits and, yes, lecturing.

The Caravan initially hit the road on February 11, 1936, traveling from Detroit to the fairgrounds in Lakeland, Florida. After that, it followed the seasons, crossing the nation's southern states in winter and heading north in the summertime. Between early 1936 and mid-1940, the Caravan of Progress covered over a million miles. It visited 251 towns and cities, not just in the United States, but also in Mexico and Cuba and was seen by some 12.5 million people.

In 1940, General Motors retired the Caravan of Progress and replaced it with a modernized road show called the Parade of Progress. For the Parade, GM built 12 entirely new, more modern-looking display vehicles called Futurliners. The main tent became larger, with an external aluminum frame and many of the exhibits were changed as well.

Opposite top - GM's Parade of Progress took over from the Caravan in mid-1940 with a new set of streamlined buses. Like the Caravan, the Parade visited an average of 60 towns and small cities each year.

Opposite bottom - GM's advance men placed ads and articles in local newspapers. When the Parade busses arrived on Main Street, everyone in town turned out. GM never charged admission, and the traveling road shows created good will for General Motors products.

The Parade's first-generation Futurliners had high-mounted bubble cabs, clamshell sides that opened and fluorescent lamp pods that cranked up seven feet above the roof. Painted red, the Futurliners' siding was distinguished by four long flutes.

The outbreak of World War II abruptly halted the Parade, especially since most of the staff joined the military. But in 1952, GM decided to send the Parade out once more. In preparation, the Futurliners were recalled for the following modifications: wraparound windshields and steel roofs replaced the bubble tops; air conditioning, power steering and self-dimming headlamps were added; paint schemes were now red and white; and the siding had seven flutes. The Parade of Progress remained in service through the middle of 1956, once again playing to thousands of Americans in small towns across the nation.

It's believed that all eight of the early Streamliners were scrapped during World War II, but nine of the 12 Futurliners survived. Three were sacrificed as donors to restore some of the others. One or two were used for a time by evangelist Oral Roberts as traveling pulpits. Another, fully restored, sold at auction for $4.3 million in January 2006.

General Motors Motoramas

Motoramas were totally separate from the Caravan/Parade of Progress. They grew out of Alfred Sloan's yearly power lunches inside New York's posh Waldorf=Astoria hotel. Sloan, GM's president and future chairman, began staging these lunches in 1931, timing them to coincide with the New York auto show each January.

Sloan traditionally invited a select group of Wall Street executives to dine with him, his intention being to let the financial community know what GM had up its sleeve for the coming year. Surrounded by GM's newest cars, Sloan would make policy announcements, sales predictions, comments about the national economy, and he'd also talk about GM's latest technical advances.

Sloan retired in 1946 but stayed active for another 10 years as chairman of the board. After World War II, General Motors expanded Sloan's guest list to include financial journalists and notables from other companies. Everyone considered it a signal honor to be invited. The list grew again in January 1949, when GM Sales and Distribution Director Spencer Hopkins suggested inviting not just the industry's movers and shakers but also, for the first time, the general public. Suddenly, the format of the gatherings changed as absolutely everyone showed up.

Workers off-load the Firebird III concept car in an
alley behind the Waldorf=Astoria in preparation for
the 1959 Motorama.

Motorama Concept Cars

1949 Transportation Unlimited:
Cadillac Caribbean, Cadillac Embassy (special paint colors), Cadillac convertible with calfskin carpets.

1950 Mid-Century Motorama:
Cadillac Debutante convertible (gold paint and brightwork, leopardskin upholstery).

1953 Motorama:
Buick Wildcat I, Buick XP-300, Cadillac Le Mans, Cadillac Orleans, Chevrolet Corvette, LeSabre, Oldsmobile Starfire X-P Rocket, Pontiac La Parisienne.

1954 Motorama:
Buick Wildcat II, Cadillac El Camino, Cadillac La Espada, Cadillac Park Avenue, Chevrolet Nomad, Chevrolet Corvair, GM Firebird XP-21, Oldsmobile F-88, Oldsmobile Cutlass, Pontiac Bonneville Special, Pontiac Strato Streak.

1955 Motorama:
Buick Wildcat III, Cadillac LaSalle II (roadster and sedan), Cadillac Eldorado Brougham, Chevrolet Biscayne, GMC L'Universelle, Oldsmobile 88 Delta, Pontiac Strato Star.

1956 Motorama:
Buick Centurion, Cadillac Eldorado Brougham towncar, Chevrolet Biscayne, Chevrolet Impala, GM Firebird II, Oldsmobile Golden Rocket, Pontiac Club de Mer.

1959 Motorama:
GM Firebird III, Pontiac X-400.

1961 Motorama:
Chevrolet Impala Special.

Concepts for Motorama

As concept cars gathered increasing rays from the Motorama limelight, Harley Earl became the event's dominant figure. Earl had studied showmanship; he had learned it from the early movie moguls back in Hollywood, where he'd grown up. Earl had lived down the street from Cecil B. DeMille, and he'd picked up cues from directors like Lubisch and von Stroheim. The resulting combination of bombast and charm nearly always let him get his way.

Earl became, in 1940, the first design director ever to be named vice president of a major auto company. He'd always counted on the patronage of Alfred Sloan, and Sloan had wisely given Earl carte blanche ever since hiring him in 1927. Nor did he disappoint Sloan. Earl built an empire within an empire on the strength of GM's financial success, much of which had to do with his cars selling well because they looked so good. General Motors led the world not only in market share but also in car design throughout Earl's 31-year tenure.

Earl had always been a great believer in advanced design. His production cars were based largely on his advanced concepts. This meant that he always kept at least one studio working on cars not for immediate production, but rather five to 10 years ahead. Earl set up an advanced studio as early as 1933, and some of those 1933 sketches and clays looked astonishingly like GM's 1939 cars.

The 1933 Cadillac V-16 Aerodynamic Coupe, shown at that year's Century of Progress in Chicago, was a running example of Earl's advanced designs, as was his 1938 Buick Y-Job and the iconic 1951 LeSabre, Earl's personal styling tour de force. Before the Motoramas gave him a stage, it probably bothered Earl that he had to keep so many of his advanced designs under wraps. The 1953 Motorama finally gave him the opportunity to show them on the grandest possible scale.

Fleets of up to 143 tractor-trailers gathered in a marshalling yard near Linden, New Jersey, to ferry exhibits and equipment to the Waldorf Motorama each year. Trucks were sent to Manhattan in sequence, and it usually took 72 solid hours of frenzy to get everything set up. After New York, Motoramas usually moved on to Boston.

Motoramas gave birth to at least two GM production cars: the 1953 Corvette and the 1957 Cadillac Eldorado Brougham. Beyond that, plenty of design details received their first public airings in Earl's concept cars—the center console, wraparound windshields, quad headlights, the fluted Nomad roof, four-door hardtops plus countless tailfin variations. Fiberglass was the material of choice for most Motorama auto bodies, and GM was the first major automaker to use it, both in and out of production. New types of powerplants, such as V-6s and gas turbines, also debuted in some of the Motorama cars.

Author Bruce Berghoff, who worked for the H.B. Stubbs Co. from 1955 to 1962, estimates that the cost per Motorama attendee rose from $2.75 in 1949 to $10.48 in 1956—and those figures didn't even include the concept cars.

Motoramas reached their peak in 1956 with seven concept cars on display and an attendance of 2.35 million. But after that season, money started getting tight, car sales dropped and GM began to rethink its Motorama strategy.

There were no shows in 1957, 1958 and 1960; the 1959 event was just a weak, next to last gasp. That Motorama played only in New York and Boston and exhibited just one true concept car, the Firebird III, powered by a gas turbine. This was one of the wildest of all the Harley Earl Motorama creations, designed by Norm James and Stefan Habsburg.

Earl himself retired at the end of 1958, and the very last Motorama took place in 1961. The 1961 show again included the Firebird III but put much greater emphasis on GM's new production cars.

Changing Priorities

It's been said that television caused the Motoramas' demise, first because people stayed home more, and second because GM found that its advertising budget could be better spent on the tube than by schlepping road shows around the country. Motoramas had become evermore expensive to produce, and GM decided that TV gave measurably more bang for the buck. So Americans bade farewell to Motoramas after 1961, although many of the major exhibits lived on after being transferred to science and technology museums in Detroit and Los Angeles.

That didn't mean, though, that General Motors stopped making and displaying concept cars. First Bill Mitchell and then Chuck Jordan made it a point to let the world know about General Motors' styling innovations. The resulting concept cars began to appear at the world's major motor shows—the exhibitions of Detroit, New York, Paris and Geneva—and even today they continue the General Motors traditions first started by Boss Kett and Mister Earl.

While the song-and-dance revues appealed to women in the audience, the cars were still the stars of the show.

Opposite - By 1959, TV had siphoned away much of the Motoramas' traditional audiences, and GM found TV ads more effective than road shows. The Firebird III turbine car became the sole concept vehicle shown that year.

The LeSabre features obvious aircraft form references, suggesting the most advanced technology. More importantly, the packaging of this design allows for a dramatically lower car. Surface development is masterful, and every detail supports the overall theme. - Stewart Reed

1953 Cadillac Le Mans

1951 Buick XP-300, 1953 Cadillac Le Mans

The Buick XP-300 and Cadillac Le Mans represent the expertise of GM styling in the early 1950s. They are used to develop distinctive brand characters and differentiation around common architecture. In this case, Cadillac and Buick interpretations are foreshadowing important design elements to come. Note the lower valance under the rear deck lid of the Cadillac. - SR

1953 Cadillac Le Mans

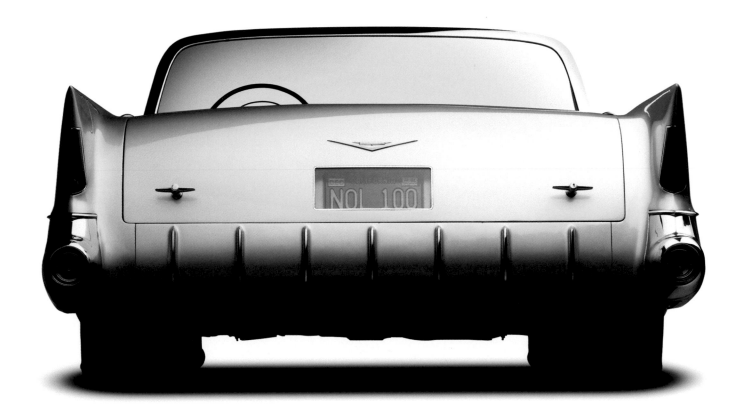

1954 Buick Wildcat II, 1954 Oldsmobile F-88

Although both the Oldsmobile and Buick styling studies use the Corvette layout as their base, they convey important differences. Notice the higher front face graphics and dual headlamps of the Buick and the very low, aggressive grille and bumper of the Olds. Also note how the F-88's hood dives lower than the fenders. – SR

1954 Buick Wildcat II

1956 Buick Centurion

The Centurion marked a huge step toward fully integrating automotive forms. All previously separate elements, such as bumpers, lamps, door handles and even transparent surfaces, now participate as total sculpture. The aircraft inspired canopy still looks futuristic to this day. - SR

1954 Firebird I, 1956 Firebird II, 1958 Firebird III

1954 Firebird I, 1956 Firebird II, 1958 Firebird III

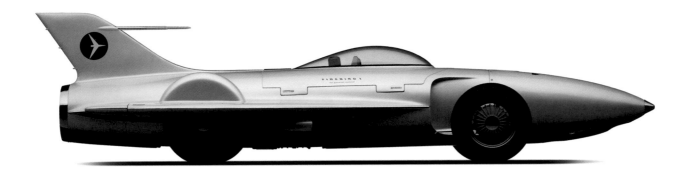

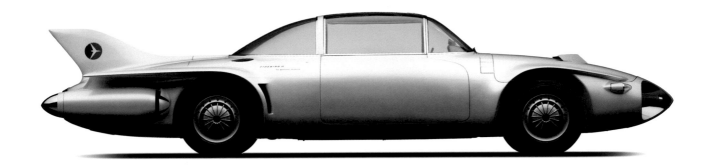

4

From Concept Car to Enduring Reality: The Corvette Story

By Jerry Burton

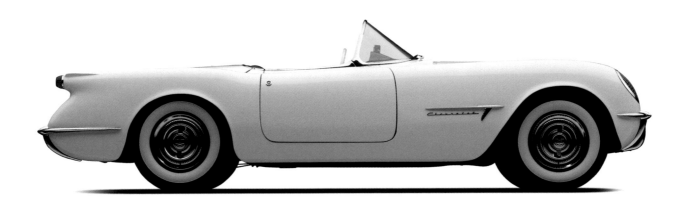

The overflow snaked down 49th Street and around the corner onto Park Avenue for another four blocks. Standing in the brisk January cold, the queue suggested a depression-era bread line. But this well-dressed crowd wasn't looking for any handouts. They were there to see what the buzz was all about inside Manhattan's Waldorf=Astoria Ballroom. The 1953 General Motors Motorama was heralding the future of the American automobile. Motorama was a precursor to the modern-day auto show, and GM had the hype machine turned on high. Amid a parade of driverless cars in motion along a hidden trolley track and precision choreography from the June Taylor dancers, there stood a glittering array of Harley Earl's newest creations.

Earl had a special small studio in a building called
Plant 8, where a small number of stylists worked on
the Corvette prototype.

The Original Corvette Studio

According to Julius Teitlebom, a model maker who worked
for Harley Earl, the original Corvette studio was housed in an
old plant about two miles east of the General Motors Building
on Grand Boulevard in Detroit. "It was a filthy, dirty studio,"
says Teitlebom, "The building, called Plant 8, was so old that
even the floor moved when you walked on it."

Both Earl and Bill Mitchell, who would replace Earl as head
of Design Staff in 1958, frequented the studio where the
Corvette clay was being shaped, and both would make
suggestions that sometimes contradicted each other.
According to Teitlebom, "Earl would come down after Mitchell
had been there and say, 'What son of a bitch did this?'"

Clare MacKichan, in a 1994 *Corvette Quarterly* interview,
remembered the period this way: "Earl kept this project
pretty much to himself. He had a special small studio with a

small number of people working on it. We all knew about it.
I don't know how many months he worked on it, but gradually,
he opened it up to the rest of us. He started with drawings,
then a clay model and a quick plaster from that."

The project had its share of problems, according to
MacKichan. "There were huge arguments about the headlights. All of us really wanted glass covers on the headlights,
but that was illegal. So we went to the fencer's mask lights.
I'm sure that we tried glass on one of the plasters, but we
couldn't make it fly with the law."

Reactions at Motorama

During the course of the week-long Motorama, the
Corvette attracted plenty of attention from people like
Dinah Shore and original NBC "Today Show" host Dave
Garroway. Wrote *Look* magazine, "The Corvette, engineered

The first production Corvettes rolled off a temporary assembly line in Flint, Michigan on June 30, 1953. Only 300 cars were made that first year, and they were all Polo white with red interiors.

by Chevrolet's Ed Cole, was the hit of the show. A Park Avenue gentleman with a mink-clad blonde on his arm surveyed the Corvette with detachment. 'You can have it darling,' the gentleman drawled, 'if it's not more than ten thousand dollars.'"

According to a Chevrolet research report dated January 1953, the Corvette was the outstanding experimental car at the show from the standpoint of practical buying interest.

The general reaction to the overall style and appearance of the Corvette was almost entirely favorable, with over 90 percent of respondents making favorable comments. Over 20 percent used superlatives in giving their opinion about it.

When visitors were asked just what it was about the car that made them like it, they gave answers like: "Unique, exciting, good advanced design, distinctive." "Best sports car I've seen." "Better than European sports cars." "[I] like the clean, well-proportioned lines and simplicity of design."

But the question remained: Could good design alone guarantee the success of an American sports car, especially one from the high-volume Big Three?

Chevrolet was about to find out. On January 19, just two days after the Corvette was shown to the press and one day after it debuted to the public, GM President Harlow Curtice announced that beginning in June, the Corvette was going into production of 300 units to be built as 1953 models.

From Curves to Wedges

While America began to undergo some profound social changes in the late 1950s, sports cars were changing, too. The voluptuous shapes of Harley Earl were evolving into something sleeker and faster. The sports car world was delighted with the fall 1961 debut of the Jaguar XKE, a modern interpretation of the famous Le Mans-winning D-Type race car– all of which meant that the new Corvette had to be spectacular in looks and performance.

As early as 1957, Mitchell was drawing inspiration for the second-generation Corvette from a series of Italian speed record cars he had spotted at the Turin Auto Show that year. "These cars all had sharp beltlines and fender blips over the wheels," said Peter Brock, a young designer in the Chevrolet studio at the time (who went on to design the Cobra Daytona Coupe). "The Alfa Romeo Disco Volantes, Fiat Abarths and several designs by . . . Stanguellini all had the same theme. Mitchell came back to Detroit with this pocket of photographs and handed them out to us in Design."

Mitchell gave his designers–Bob Veryzer, Chuck Pohlman and Brock–several weeks to see what they could come up with. Each man drew his own sketch, but one of the sketches blew Mitchell away. It featured a high beltline with an outward crease around the perimeter of the car, a sharp, pointed nose and a fastback roofline. "He picked that one sketch of mine down off the wall," said Brock, "I was the lucky guy who got to draw it, but Mitchell picked out the theme he wanted to follow."

Brock's original design featured several innovations that never made it into the street car, including the elimination of the A-pillar. "Mitchell wanted to do 'something really different' with the glass area, taking it way past the wrap-around windscreens that were so much in vogue at that time," said Brock.

While Mitchell had his team pursue other directions for the second-generation Corvette body, he knew deep down that Brock had nailed it. The next iteration of that theme was the Q Corvette, an engineering concept involving a front engine linked to a rear-mounted transmission via a torque tube. The wedge-shaped body Mitchell commissioned was sleek and beautiful, but tooling cost issues and corporate preoccupation with the upcoming 1960 debut of the Corvair worked against the Q's production.

Mitchell's next move was to commission the same wedge-shape theme into a race car body for the Corvette SS mule chassis, which had been dormant since GM withdrew from racing. Mitchell had purchased the chassis for a nominal fee and had plans to conduct his own racing effort with driver Dick Thompson.

The race car became the Sting Ray Racer. Like its name-sake sea creature, the race car redesign had much of its character on the upper surfaces. The wedge-shape was distinguished by a pointed edge that ran around the perimeter of the car, touching the tops of the fender wells. The relatively flat upper surfaces were punctuated by high

arches to accommodate the wheels. Originally finished in red, it was later repainted Lucite Silver and given a silver leather interior.

Mitchell was determined to move forward on a production Corvette based on his Sting Ray racer and in the fall of 1959, he commissioned Larry Shinoda to execute its adaptation. "It was the best way to go," said Brock. ". . . we had time to refine it, but it didn't become bland or watered down. Somehow, we were able to retain that original freshness."

Besides Chuck Pohlman, Gene Garfinkel and Larry Shinoda were brought in to help translate the theme into a production version, with Shinoda handling much of the detailing such as the hoodvents and double cockpit. The street prototype was called XP-720 and Mitchell had plans for a coupe and a convertible.

Battle Over the Split Window

While Corvette engineer Zora Arkus-Duntov and his team were working on the chassis for the XP-720, which included an independent rear suspension, Mitchell had something else up his sleeve. He wanted to incorporate a tapered, boattail hardtop with a wind split running from the nose of the car to the tail in a relatively uninterrupted line. That line would form a split window at the rear, a design cue that had originally surfaced in the 1937 Bugatti Type 57 SC Atlantic and on the 1956 Oldsmobile Golden Rocket show car.

Duntov had been aware of Mitchell's plan for a coupe. But when he first saw the tapered fastback roofline with the split window, he was aghast. Such an intrusion would severely interfere with rearward visibility. Duntov later recalled seeing the first prototype of the XP-720 in the GM styling dome with Bill Mitchell. "We are sitting there, and Bill was squinting at the car and said, 'Ah, look at it. You see the blood, the blood streaming out of the mouth of the car–like big fish.'"

Duntov later referred to the blood as "my blood." The discussion deteriorated into a name-calling battle, then threats by Mitchell to coerce GM management into pulling the plug on technology that Duntov held dear, such as independent rear suspension. Duntov simply didn't have the corporate clout to go up against the likes of Mitchell. So he took his battle to Ed Cole, who decided to let Mitchell have his split window, at least for the first year. Duntov earned the larger victory, however, and the split disappeared altogether after 1963.

The Third Generation

Bill Mitchell based the third-generation Corvette on the Mako Shark II show car. The Mako II was an even more ostentatious version of Mako Shark I, a shark-themed body built over the chassis of a first-generation Corvette. While

When it came time to translate the Sting Ray
theme into a production version, the result was the
XP-720 prototype. Shown on the patio courtyard at
the GM Design Center, it was used here to evaluate
various bumper designs.

When compared to the 1982 C3, the all-new 1984
C4 Corvette at right bore a family resemblance
although it was shorter and wider with straighter
and sleeker fender lines. These changes enabled a
drag coefficient of 0.34, nearly 25 percent better
than its older sibling.

it maintained the same shark-like paint job as its predecessor, the Mako II featured flared appendages and high, arching fenders above huge turbine blade wheels with knock-off hubs. It had a tapered fastback roofline with louvers, a James Bond 007-style revolving license plate, a retractable rear bumper and a rear spoiler.

Mitchell built the Mako II in 1965 as a potential 1967 production car and battled once again with Duntov over its configuration as the third-generation Corvette. Duntov, of course, was set on a mid-engined design and objected to Mitchell's penchant for long hoods and short rear decks.

But Mitchell, who clearly carried more clout than Duntov when it came to the design of GM's sacred cow, triumphed again. The non-running show car debuted at the New York Auto Show in April 1965. By October, a fully operational Mako II powered by a 427 cubic inch engine was shown at the Paris Auto Show.

While Mitchell wanted to build a production version of the Mako II, Duntov was successful in having the new car delayed for a year while toning down the high arching fenders in an effort to improve visibility. The third-generation car would last 15 model years. By 1975, when Zora Arkus-Duntov retired and was replaced by Dave McLellan, America's appetite for the Corvette was well established.

Generation Four

After Bill Mitchell retired in 1977, Irv Rybicki took the reins at Design Staff. Rybicki gave his individual studio designers more autonomy, which allowed Chevrolet studio head Jerry Palmer to execute a fourth-generation Corvette design without interference. Palmer sought a more precise and purposeful shape. "We concentrated on basics like cleanliness, comfort and function," said Palmer.

But Palmer also understood the necessity of maintaining an instantly identifiable Corvette look. "The car had to show the bloodlines of the great predecessors," said Palmer. "The lineage of the Corvette had to be very apparent." (*Corvette Quarterly*, Winter 1996, page 33.)

Palmer had designed the last mid-engined Corvettes built under Duntov's tenure—the XP-880, the Reynolds Aluminum Corvette and the Aerovette. He parked the Aerovette inside the studio for reference during much of the fourth-generation development as he reinterpreted its lines into a front-engined machine with a blunt Kamm tail.

While maintaining a distinct resemblance to these earlier cars, the initial fourth-generation clays retained the long hood and short deck of previous Corvettes. But the fender lines were straighter and sleeker. Contributing to this effect was a windshield that had been moved forward with a 64-degree rake.

Working with McLellan and Palmer, designer John Cafaro sketched out a giant clamshell hood as early as 1978, which showcased the underpinnings of the entire front end. "I probably spent as much time on that engine compartment as I did on the whole exterior," said Palmer. "I'm still proud of that because it set the standard for the rest of GM cars." (*Corvette Quarterly*, Winter 1996, Page 33.)

A perimeter break line ran around the body, rising slightly from front to rear. The rear design preserved the Corvette classic twin-round taillights motif, while the front maintained the trademark hidden headlamps.

Because Dave McLellan was devoted to making more of a pure engineering statement with the new machine, wind tunnel testing was conducted in GM's new 4,000 hp wind tunnel. The effort paid off with a drag coefficient of 0.34, nearly 25 percent better than the 1982 Corvette.

The fourth-generation body turned out to be nine inches shorter than the 1982 Corvette and two inches wider, which created a roomier interior. Reversing the trend, the fourth-generation wheelbase was actually two inches shorter than its predecessor's.

The fourth-generation Corvette was launched in 1983 as a 1984 model and lasted through 1996. The C4 era also saw the launch of a special widebody ZR-1 model, which set a new benchmark for Corvette performance with a 32-valve overhead cam V-8 built in association with Lotus. Sadly, the ZR-1 languished on the market. After initially high demand upon its debut for the 1990 model year, it was discontinued in 1995.

Generation Five

John Cafaro would head up the fifth-generation Corvette design team, reporting to Jerry Palmer. In creating the finished design, thousands of concepts were rendered on sketchpads and computers, the more promising ones becoming scale clays. Some clays were fully mocked up but had different design treatments on each side; these were known as "clown suits."

Meanwhile, engineering under the leadership of Dave McLellan had developed a radical new architecture for the fifth-generation Corvette; a full perimeter frame with hydro-formed side rails and a central backbone structure. It was enormously stiff, which made it possible to not only tune the suspension more precisely, but also allowed for a convertible without extra structural reinforcement. However, early in the C5's development, chief engineer Dave McLellan retired and was succeeded by Dave Hill.

Meanwhile, the emerging C5 shape featured a low hood line made possible by a more compact LS1 V-8 engine. Great visibility had never been a hallmark for these cars, but the C5 offered the best frontal visibility ever on a Corvette, enabling an average-sized driver to view an object that was 18 feet closer to the front bumper than in the C4.

According to John Cafaro, "The C5's body is as smooth as you can get because we shaped it in a wind tunnel within tenths of millimeters to achieve a .29 drag coefficient. We worked so hard that if you were to change anything the slightest bit, the aero numbers would increase."

Corvette's trademark four round taillights remained on the C5, although the lamps themselves became oval-shaped. The word "Corvette" was embossed in an italicized font across the rear fascia, under which the four exhaust outlets converged.

For the first time ever, the Corvette was offered in three body styles—T-top coupe, convertible and a fixed-roof coupe introduced in 1999 that later became the reincarnation of the ultra-high performance Z06.

The C5 represented a quantum leap in both performance and practicality thanks to its intelligent architecture and rigid structure. It enjoyed a run of eight very successful model years.

Generation Six

Unlike previous generations, the fifth-generation car was at the top of its game when work began on a sixth-generation car. Tom Peters was the lead exterior designer for the C6. "The C5 was a spectacular car and a hard act to follow," said Peters. "But I also had some ideas where I thought the car

should be going. A tighter, smaller car. Leaner. That was key." The C6 would be 5.1 inches shorter in length and 1.0 inch narrower in width. The wheelbase, however, was increased by 1.1 inches to create a smoother ride, reduce overhangs and accommodate a new automatic transmission that would debut in 2006.

Although there were subtle elements of past Corvettes that could be worked in, the designers of the C6 did not want to do a retro car according to Peters. More important than heritage was the inspiration found in fighter jet aircraft. "Really, the C6 upper body is inspired by the F-22 Raptor canopy," explained Peters.

Given the new Corvette's projected performance parameters, with top speeds well in excess of 180 mph, the final design needed to cut through the air with minimal drag. After over 400 hours in the wind tunnel, an incredibly low 0.286 drag coefficient was achieved. Contributing to the low drag number were fixed, exposed headlamps, a major break from Corvette tradition.

The sixth-generation cars debuted in fall 2004. A higher performance Z06 version followed a year later, which maintained the coupe's body style with a fixed roof panel, wide fender flares, aluminum frame and the abundant use of carbon fiber.

Tom Wallace succeeded Dave Hill in early 2007 as chief engineer and vehicle line executive–only to turn chief engineer duties over to Tadge Juechter a few months later. For the ultimate Corvette, Wallace continued Hill's plans for a supercharged rocket sled code-named Blue Devil. The 638 hp supercar, with its extensive use of visible carbon fiber and Brembo carbon ceramic matrix brakes, will set a new performance benchmark for a GM production car; a power-to-weight ratio of 5.2 pounds per horsepower and a certified top speed of 205 mph. In late summer 2008, at roughly the same time GM was celebrating its 100th anniversary, the Blue Devil debuted as the 2009 ZR1. And the beat goes on.

The sixth-generation Corvette was unveiled in January 2004. Although subtle elements of past Corvettes were integrated into the design, its designers did not wish to create a retro car. New inspiration was found in fighter jet aircraft. In fact, the upper body was based on a F-22 Raptor.

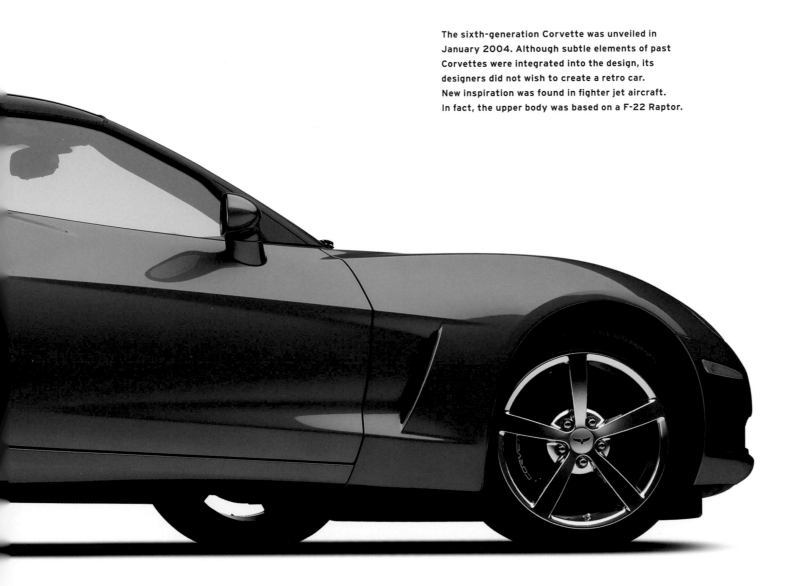

Two-Seat Fantasies and Reality
by Jerry Burton

Two-seaters were never the exclusive province of Chevrolet. Cadillac, Buick, Oldsmobile and Pontiac all created two-seat concept vehicles, going back to the original Motoramas, and all but Oldsmobile have ventured into the production two-seater market. Most of these efforts have been short-lived, although three different two-seaters were still in production at the time of GM's Centennial.

After showing the Wildcat I at the 1953 Motorama, Buick returned with a much sportier Wildcat II in 1954, with flying-wing fenders that flared straight out from the body, exposing a chromed front suspension. Pontiac countered with its own bubble-topped Bonneville Special, Cadillac showed a two-seat hardtop called the El Camino and even Oldsmobile got into the act with its F-88 two-seater, which featured a 324 cid V-8 engine nestled into a Corvette chassis.

After the 1954 Motorama show, the other divisions soon left the two-seat market to Chevrolet, although a two-seat LaSalle II was shown in 1955 and previewed the side coves that would appear on the 1956 Corvette.

It wasn't until 1964 that Pontiac came back with a Banshee showcar based on the third-generation Corvette then undergoing development. The Banshee was created at the behest of Pontiac General Manager John DeLorean and was said to weigh some 500 pounds less than the Corvette, but senior GM management deemed it too much of a threat to the Chevrolet.

From 1968 through 1973, GM's German subsidiary, Opel, offered the Opel GT that was styled loosely after the third-generation Corvette. In the United States, all Opels were available through Buick dealers.

It wasn't until the 1984 model year that Pontiac would have its own production two-seater, the Pontiac Fiero. Code-named the P Car, this mid-engined creation was sold internally as a high-mileage commuter car that showcased plastic skin and revolutionary construction methods. It was engineered under the direction of Turkish-born Hulki Aldikacti. Given its mid-engined configuration, many expected sports car performance and were disappointed by the Fiero's 2.5-liter four-cylinder 92 hp engine and less-than-stellar handling.

The Fiero was designed by John Schinella and Ron Hill, with a final tweaking by Pontiac Design Chief Jack Humbert, the man responsible for the trademark Pontiac look going back to the early 1960s.

The Fiero didn't really begin to command the respect of sports car people until a 2.8-liter V-6-powered version, the Fiero GT, was launched in 1985, followed by a facelift in 1986. By then it was too late, as competitors such as the Toyota MR2 and Honda CRX had eroded the Fiero's market. The Fiero was discontinued after the 1988 model year.

In 1986, Buick showed a mid-engined Wildcat concept car powered by an overhead cam V-6. But the car was never seriously considered for production.

The following year, Cadillac launched an ambitious luxury sports car called the Allanté, which was designed to compete against that favorite country club two-seater, the Mercedes-Benz SL.

In a historic first, General Motors bid out the Allanté design project, pitting the in-house GM Design staff against Pininfarina of Italy. Pininfarina won amid much bad blood. The resulting Allanté design was cleanly sculpted but not boldly Cadillac. The chassis was a shortened version of the front-wheel drive 1986 Eldorado underpinnings, complete with Cadillac's aluminum V-8 and related transaxle.

In an unusual move, it was decided to airship the chassis from Detroit's Hamtramck plant to Italy for body installation and then back to Detroit for final assembly. The costs were enormous.

The Allanté struggled in the marketplace. At first, Cadillac tried to tie resale value to the Mercedes SL, then to other prestige nameplates. Although dealers did a brisk business with return customers taking advantage of the guaranteed resale, it was a financial disaster for General Motors.

There was one surprise left for the Allanté's last model year of 1993. That year, Cadillac installed the all-new, high-performance Northstar V-8 in the final run of Allantés—and

Following the success of the Corvette at the 1953 Motorama, GM's other divisions were soon to create their own two-seat concepts. Shown here is the 1954 bubble-topped Pontiac Bonneville Special.

After the 1954 Motorama show, and poor sales for the first Corvettes, GM's other divisions quickly decided to leave the two-seat market to Chevrolet. One exception was the LaSalle II concept car shown in 1955. Although the car did not lead to a revival of the extinct marque, this prototype did preview the side coves that would appear on the 1956 Corvette.

one unit was chosen to pace the 2003 Indianapolis 500. It was a proud moment for a curiously international two-seat Cadillac that never found a market.

The 1988 model year brought forth a Buick two-seater, the Reatta, which was initially available as a coupe only. Designed and built at the Lansing Craft Center, the Reatta was visually unexceptional, looking a lot like a cut-down 1986 Riviera. However, the Reatta did find a small niche of buyers who appreciated the luxurious appointments, the sure-footed front-wheel drive and the torquey and relatively bulletproof 3800 V-6 engine.

The first Reatta ragtop arrived in 1990 and removing the fixed roof positively transformed the appearance. To many, the smooth, soft lines of the Reatta—particularly the convertible—were more appealing than the cold, chiseled style of the Allanté. But the convertible was late and expensive. The Reatta disappeared after the 1991 model year.

Despite abandoning the Allanté in 1993, Cadillac had learned valuable lessons in the process. Dave Hill, former chief engineer of the Allanté, had since become Corvette chief engineer. And Hill knew he had the perfect platform for a resurrected Cadillac sports car—the rigid structure of the fifth- and sixth-generation Corvette.

Meanwhile, Cadillac had shown the Evoq show car at the 1999 Detroit International Auto Show to rave reviews. Designed by Kip Wosenko and Tom Peters, the power-hard-toped convertible was absolutely stunning with its chiseled, faceted design, which defined an emerging Cadillac look.

Production of the new two-seat XLR commenced in the 2004 model year. In 2007, the XLR high performance V-Series was added to the lineup, and the XLR remains in production today as a halo for the Cadillac division.

When Bob Lutz became product chief of GM in 2001, one of his first moves was to create an attractive and affordable sports car—a $20,000 competitor to the perennial favorite, the Mazda Miata. The result was the Pontiac Solstice shown at the Detroit auto show in 2002.

The Solstice, which has a clear Pontiac identity, is powered by an energetic 170 hp 2.4-liter overhead cam engine with variable valve timing. The car went into production in 2005 as a 2006 model. It was built on the Kappa architecture, which was predicated on small production runs with a relatively low initial investment. The Saturn Division created its own distinctive version, the Sky, in the 2006 model year.

A high-performance GXP version of the Solstice, powered by a turbocharged 2.0 Liter Ecotech, debuted as a 2007 model. Saturn simultaneously introduced a similar version called the Red Line.

While the Corvette continues to dominate the two-seat story at General Motors, the other divisions appear to have learned valuable lessons from the Corvette's success. Performance must accompany design when it comes to generating market loyalty.

1952 Chevrolet Corvette EX-122

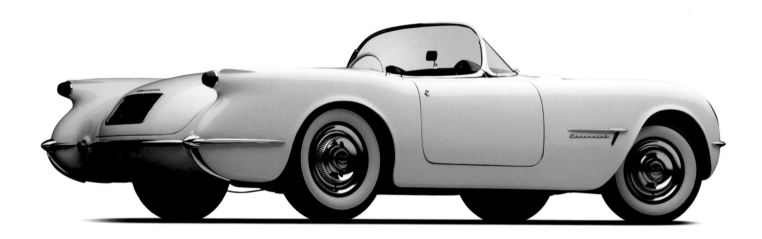

A thoroughly athletic looking car, the Corvette prototype
has a lean, pure shape and open wheel cuts emphasizing its
large wheels. Crafted in a new material, the forms express
its molded construction with a smooth, seamless surface.
- Stewart Reed

1959 Sting Ray Racer

The very dynamic wide line surrounding the Sting Ray creates
tremendous tension and sharply defines the light-to-shadow
change. The sculptural forms of fenders, hood and headrest
beautifully contrast the edges. – SR

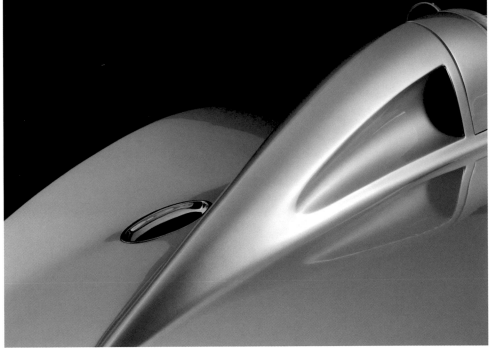

1961 Mako Shark I

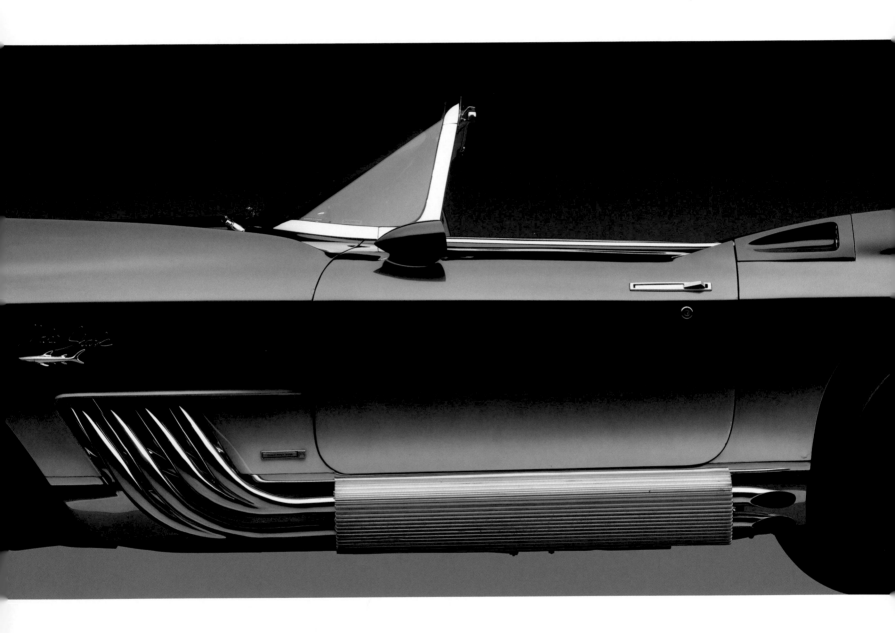

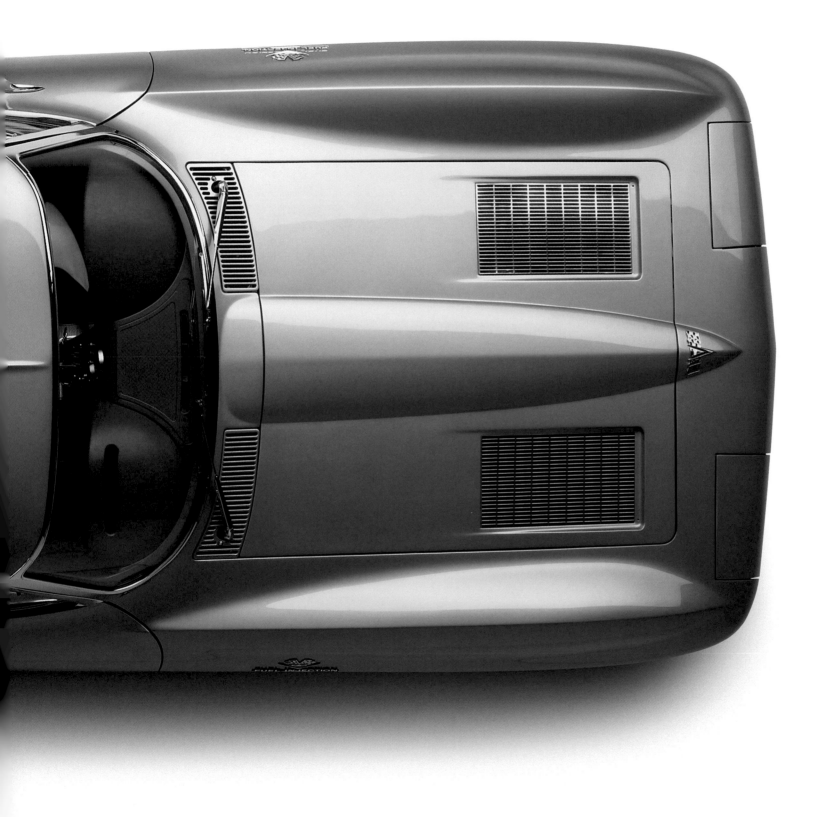

1967 Corvette Sting Ray Roadster

A masterful evolution and refinement of the essential theme developments of the Sting Ray race car (page 144) and the Mako Shark I (page 148). The Corvette Sting Ray is one of the most successful designs ever and evidence of the value of concept vehicles in setting a clear path for production cars.
- SR

1967 Corvette Sting Ray Coupe

1965 Mako Shark II

The dramatic proportion of the Mako Shark II is achieved by
sharply creased fender forms, which originate low (both at
the front and the low waistline) and leap dramatically over
the wheels. Also unique is the wrap-around glass surface from
windshield to side. – SR

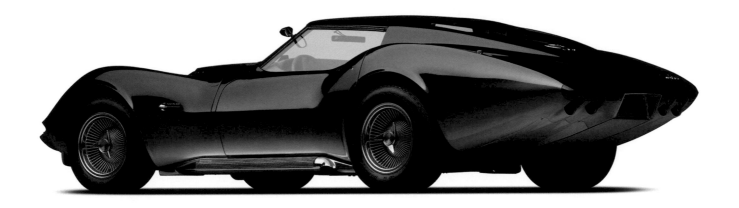

1969 Corvette Stingray

2009 C6 Corvette ZR1

5

Reaching for the Sky:
The Rise and Fall of the Tailfin

By Tracy Powell

Following World War II, the United States was inundated with futuristic design, much of which included aircraft styling cues. The optimistic consumer culture embraced this new and far-reaching direction, particularly as it related to automobiles. The specters of future modes of personal transportation were promoted by *Popular Science* and *Popular Mechanics*, and it seemed only a matter of time before "flying cars" would populate the air space. Hovercraft was a hot area of research, originating in the confines of military application and drifting into the public sphere. With optimistic visions of a semi-utopian technological future, the sky was literally the limit.

In the economic boom years following World War II, potential car buyers, as well as the curious public, eagerly awaited new models. When automakers unveiled their new wares, it was a real event, and crowds flocked to dealerships to see new cars such as Buick's 1956 offerings.

From 1938 until 1956, General Motors published an in-house magazine for their employees called *GM Folks*. This cover from November of 1942 illustrates a number of U.S. warplanes, many of which GM produced as part of the war effort. When hostilities ceased, Harley Earl's designers took inspiration from the shapes of these aircraft.

It was only logical that the intertwined ideas of personal transport and ground-based pragmatism would result in styling that included tailfins. As Norm James, designer of GM's Firebird III concept vehicle, noted, "It should not be that unusual that if aircraft were to start looking like cars then cars should start looking like aircraft. After a while, the fins started to be associated with 'being new.' No cars were built during the war so we expected that after a few missed years, new designs had some catching up to do."

And catch up they did, every year leading up to September and October, which was when automakers all unveiled their new wares. In those days, free coffee, donuts and balloons for the kids were handed out at the dealerships as lots stayed open late. New models in the showroom, replete with sheet metal that often changed each season, were the main attraction at these events. The breakneck pace and constant competition kept stylists, product planners and engineers running, as their cars had only a 12-month shelf life. The automobile industry's brisk pace of new seasonal offerings

seemed to rival the fashion business with its out-with-the-old, in-with-the-new zeal to attract new buyers and capture a greater share of the market.

Looking to the Sky

For auto makers, "in-with-the-new" meant radical departures from prewar offerings. Kaiser-Frazier created cars that no longer had fenders. Tucker developed "aircraft apparent" front ends. Studebaker made cars that looked like they were "driving backwards." Everyone fully expected new cars to look quite different, and General Motors was no exception. Although Detroit's Big Three lagged behind the independents in new post-war design, GM jumped to the front with bold statements in 1948, showcasing the brilliant new Cadillacs and the Futuramic Oldsmobile 98s.

Inside GM's Styling department, the goal was to design elements that had impact. Along with the use of large bullet noses, spinners and other aircraft-inspired features, came the tailfin. In fact, these elements weren't exactly new to

The restyled 1948 Cadillac is considered the first American automobile with tailfins. This early clay design study clearly shows the introduction of these aircraft-inspired shapes at the rear of the car.

GM designers, as they had been drawn up and used on scale models before the war. GM design chief Harley Earl was first captivated by the Lockheed P-38 "Lightning" fighter plane, to which he had taken a group of about 30 colleagues to observe, just before America entered World War II. The P-38 was a twin-fuselaged, single-wing fighter with a canopy in the center; the two fuselages had dual fins.

The plane's streamlining and individuality stamped an indelible impression on Earl and others, and facets of the P-38's twin tails and booms were incorporated into later post-war designs, most noticeably the 1948 Cadillac's "fish tails." The standoffish attitude of many Cadillac dealers, who were fearful of a design lemon, soon changed when sales proved strong; buyers related the new treatment to prestige and distinctiveness.

The reason that Cadillac sported the first fins—and why they reached their zenith a decade later on Cadillacs—was differentiation. When it came to models throughout the GM divisions, great thought had been given to the desirability of

clear-cut identification. And Cadillac's fins were an instant symbol of recognition. When Alfred Sloan first saw the new postwar Cadillac during test runs at the GM Proving Ground, he called over John F. Gordon, then general manager of the division, squeezed his arm, and is said to have commented: "Now, Jack, you have a Cadillac in the rear as well as the front."

The restyle of 1948 applied to the Cadillac Sixty Special, Series 61 and 62 and later to the entire line. The "fish tails" remained intact and virtually unchanged over the next four years, and the division's loyal customer base responded well. Sales increased throughout these years, even in 1951, when the U.S. government capped production during the Korean conflict.

Optimism and Exploration

The story of early postwar Cadillac parallels the story of the United States in the 1950s: The same thread of unbridled optimism stamped on America at the time was seen in the advent of the tailfin. As that optimism grew, so did the fins.

The era of abundance that had begun in the 1940s had, by 1959, reached proportions that were fantastic by any previous standards. Nearly a half-trillion dollars' worth of goods and services were being produced by the U.S. economy.

In addition, the 1950s were a period of experimentation; entertainment was revolutionized by the mainstream introduction of television, rapid growth of the recording industry, new genres of music and movies targeted at teenage audiences. The sexual revolution also took root in the 1950s (Hugh Hefner launched *Playboy* magazine in 1953), and some automotive styling elements hinted at promiscuity, such as the so-called artillery-shell-shaped "Dagmar" bumper overriders, so named after a buxom TV personality. More specifically, tailfins pointed toward modernism, as well as animalistic traits.

"That was back in the days when, if the customer wanted backup lights—little, pointed beehive spheres—they were bolted to the back of the car," said Irv Rybicki, who was working in the Cadillac studio at the time and would become GM Design Staff Vice President. "We carried fins in '49, and, in '50 we were looking to change the fins."

Thanks to Cadillac's "fish tails," which remained through the 1955 model year—Cadillacs were selling so well, executives saw no reason to change—fins became a calling card for luxury branding. The division had long planned to become the country's premiere luxury marque, and by mid-decade, aided by advanced engineering and evolutionary design, Cadillac commanded a 55 percent share of the luxury market.

The division chose 1955 to introduce a new styling element, one that evolved from the smaller fin/taillight assembly; sharply pointed "shark" fins now appeared on the Eldorado. That year, Cadillac set an all-time sales record, moving 140,777 cars out of its show rooms.

But by 1957, Cadillac's fins were too popular to relegate to just one division. The extent to which they were imitated, both inside the corporation and out, is evidence of their design virtue. Inside GM, Buick had already dabbled with the concept of fender top appendages on its 1954 Skylark. In 1957, Chevrolet adapted fins, accentuated by arcing side trim, for the first time and featured eye-catching duo-tone paint schemes, a design foray that began in 1954. Outside GM, Virgil Exner led Chrysler's push with attractive and well-integrated fin-based designs.

Blessed Excess

In 1956 GM stylist Chuck Jordan, who would follow Rybicki as GM Design Staff Vice President, happened upon Chrysler's new 1957 models arrayed in a parking lot and in full view. Jordan quickly realized that Exner's "Forward Look" designs surpassed GM's and hurried back to the studios, where he described the models to Mitchell and anyone else who would listen. It didn't take long for scores of other stylists to drive down to take a look as well.

"Our friends in Highland Park came out with some fins that were a foot and a half over the fender crown lines, and that put fear in the GM design staff, so we did wild fins, rockets and tubes," said Rybicki. "I often sat back when all of this was happening and wondered where we would go from there, because that was pretty far out."

According to Norm James, the popularity of the tailfin was "no different from today's cars that have shaped, stylish head and taillight assemblies and have adapted certain modern proportions. This is what people see and accept as a present-day style. In the 1950s, everyone, including designers, thought they [fins] looked neat. They kept getting bigger and bigger and then Chrysler entered the fin game with some success and raised the stakes, as I think—proportionally—they were integrating them better with the body, rather than adding them as appendages."

It was during this time of intense competition with Chrysler that GM purchased several Chrysler models and painted them a solid clay color, glass and all, for evaluation as clay models. GM sought to discover what made their competitor's models so successful. "It's not that unusual that people liked fins," James added, "as the mantra at Styling was to find new ways of doing windshield pillars, three-quarter rear panels and rocker panel sections—finding a different way of doing something was very highly valued and they promised (unspoken) rewards to those that could come up with original solutions."

Cadillacs of 1957 vintage are often considered the most dramatic-looking cars in the division's postwar history. On the first line of that short list was the over-the-top Eldorado Brougham, a descendent of a trio of show cars: the Orleans, the Park Avenue and the Brougham. Elsewhere in the lineup, sexy Sixty Specials, sleek, tailfinned Series 62s and formal 75s joined the Eldorado Seville and Biarritz convertible.

Fins were in, especially for the jet set and frequent travelers, ubiquitous to the point of infiltrating American society as much as suspected Communists. In one telling "Sputnik moment" in 1957 (after news broke of the Soviets orbiting the first space satellite), Senator Styles Bridges admonished Americans to "be less concerned with . . . the height of the tailfin on the new car and prepared to shed blood, sweat and tears if this country and the free world are to survive."

As time progressed, the excesses of the 1950s were reflected in the increasing size of tail fins. Cadillac's tailfin, which began life as little more than a subtle, neat exercise

Top - This 1957 Cadillac advertisement depicts two of the most dramatic-looking cars in the division's post-war history, the over-the-top Eldorado Brougham sedan and the Biarritz convertible. Both of these models show strong relationships with earlier Motorama show cars and have become favorites of collectors today.

Middle - This *GM Folks* issue from 1953 shows various General Motors models displayed around a U.S. Air Force jet. With this cover, an obvious direct comparison is being made between automobiles and aircraft of the jet age.

Bottom - Buick brochures for 1958 emphasized the ornate and costly grille and front-end treatment of the company's new models.

in 1948, grew bolder with time, and by the end of the Motoramas, the era of tailfin had run its course. The trend lasted as long as it did because it was simply a matter of consumer satisfaction. GM gave the public what it wanted.

It was with the tailfin that Harley Earl showed his uncanny ability to predict what would sell. And he was right on target. With the exception of the 1958 recession, GM carved an ever-increasing slice of market share thanks, in large part, to the corporation's new styling direction. The fins were part and parcel of this success, even to the point of setting a new trend, however short-lived it was. By the same token, Exner led his group at Chrysler, producing a range of attractive tail-finned and streamlined models that created a stir wherever they were seen. One can only speculate what Chrysler would have accomplished if the quality of its cars had equaled their looks.

This isn't to say that tall tailfins were admired by all. GM's 1958 model year has been maligned as the worst across-the-board design effort in memory, and hastily contrived tailfins were much to blame. One example was the '58 Buick with its monstrous, costly grille and front-end treatment and over-done, chrome-tipped fins. At Pratt Institute in New York, where GM stylist Norm James cut his teeth, a good approach to automotive styling meant putting fins on cars simply because, as James said, "cars looked good with fins. The non-automotive design community, however, looked down on these popular styles." Purists considered the fins outlandish, too flamboyant to be taken seriously. "[But] when Harley Earl [told] us that he wanted something that looked like a floozy from Las Vegas, we understood that if we didn't put fins on it, someone else would."

Ed Glowacke was Cadillac's design chief in the late 1950s, and his push for an innovative design to quash Chrysler led to work that began in the fall of 1956 on the '59 Cadillac. This model is best known for its towering fins, the apex of this concept at GM.

The '59 Cadillac, with dual bullet taillamps mounted on each fin, joined a horde of other outlandish-looking cars sporting high-flying fins and decadent amounts of chrome and color. The contest between GM and Chrysler to hit the high-fin mark set Chevrolets and Cadillacs against Plymouths and Imperials. The Buicks of 1959 were sculpted with clean, crisp lines, "delta wing" tailfins and modest amounts of brightwork along the doors and fenders. Pontiac called its heavily chromed fins "bunny ears." And as high as fins reached on Cadillacs, fins on Chevrolets spread out from the rear center line to create a "batwing" tail. On paper, the broad, flat fins had enough surface area to cause the rear end to lift if the car was traveling fast enough–more than 100 mph–which was, fortunately, not possible.

Lost in the shadows of this forest of fins, however, small cars were enjoying a greater share of the market than ever before. This was not lost on Bill Mitchell, who had taken over for Earl and was already planning a different styling direction. A decade after the fins came into play, Mitchell and others in the studios were on a quest to play them down and take design down a more "slender" path. Ironically,- it was Mitchell, along with other stylists, including Frank Hershey, who promoted fins in the first place. When these details first appeared on the 1948 Cadillac, Mitchell had referred to them as "little nubbins." Perhaps his intuition should be credited for accurately understanding that tastes change with time. The battle of the tailfin had ended almost as quickly as it had erupted

Mitchell, who considered the current design direction heavy and dated, took advantage of Earl's absence during a trip to Europe to push new designs that played down the use–or misuse–of chrome and other elements. The clay models that were developed would become the sleek and lean cars of 1959. Yes, they had fins, but the new cars were restrained and well received by consumers.

The 1959 Cadillac was the high water mark for the tailfin. Here designers are shown working on the roofline of a full-scale illustration of a sedan. By the time the '59 model year approached, tailfins were already beginning to fall out of favor.

James recalls the period of the tailfin's fall as coinciding with the completion of the Firebird III in 1959. "Earl or someone else directed that the master plaster model of the FB III be put into the Cadillac studio for inspiration, and it appears that the lower fins/skegs over the '61 Cadillac rear wheels were a direct result of that. Fins started disappearing about the time that Bill Mitchell took over Styling and after our Firebird III had worn out its introduction."

The economic downturn of 1958, which saw both sales and profits in the auto manufacturing sector unexpectedly nosedive, resulted in much hand-wringing among auto executives as the 1959 model year approached. Tailfins, now considered the embodiment of excess, seemed unnecessary, even unflattering.

Clipped Fins

The first hint that Cadillac's fins were on their way out was the downscaling that began on the 1960 models. Mitchell had moved young Chuck Jordan to the Cadillac studio in 1958 to revolutionize the look of GM's top line. The '60 Cadillac Sixty Special was lower, sleeker and featured scaled-back Chevrolet-like horizontal fins. Later models featured a shorter fin on top of a rounded, trailing body, tell-tale signs that the fin was losing favor. The fins on '64 Cadillacs were miniscule, and by the next model year they were gone. Buicks of 1960 were also finless. Beginning with the 1961 model year, the move away from fins hit Chevrolet; Mitchell sheared off all but implied traces of fins, replacing them with a clean boattail with a squared rear panel.

"When we had those [finned cars] on the road, most of us decided we were moving away from automobiles into other forms that none of us really understood," Rybicki said. "So, Bill [Mitchell], in his wisdom, decided we'd better start cleaning up our act. We got rid of the fins and started moving back toward automotive shapes. Bill was a fellow who liked hard-edged cars, and he had to have creases in fenders and uppers, so we were taking a different direction. Earl came from the school of round, and Bill Mitchell was more toward the shear."

The de-finning of GM models appeared to work. In 1962, selling to the largest car market in history with a litany of new products, GM hit record production for all five divisions, and Chevrolet had its first two-million-car year. The following year set new highs, and Mitchell's new styling direction, devoid of fins for the most part, was ingrained throughout the company.

"The irony is that when fins were removed from cars, they were and are still considered 'politically incorrect' and no designer dares to re-introduce them," James said. "I'm not saying they should return, but just that, as they were rejected by the Industrial Design profession in my day, the stigma remains." Indeed, fins faded from sight and eventually disappeared during Mitchell's watch. Mitchell considered the apex of the tailfin, seen on 1958-1959 models, the "worst" design element during his tenure at General Motors.

"In '58 we were putting the chrome on with a trowel," Mitchell said. "So, when I took over, my job was to get them down, and I did. I cleaned them down. But I've got to say this—they had some identity."

The de-finning of GM models appeared to work, because by 1962 record production was reached in all divisions. This advertisement clearly shows Bill Mitchell's new styling direction with a "clipped fin" Cadillac.

Cadillac supremacy

Wherever highways lead and quality is recognized, Cadillac is known and accepted as motordom's supreme achievement.

VISIT YOUR LOCAL AUTHORIZED CADILLAC DEALER

1949 Buick Roadmaster Convertible

1949 Buick Roadmaster Convertible, 1949 Buick Super Estate Wagon

1953 Cadillac Eldorado, 1953 Oldsmobile Fiesta, 1953 Buick Skylark

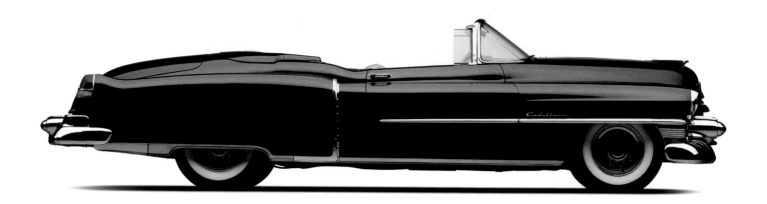

Each brand bears distinctive traits: the Oldsmobile (top right) features a dynamic diagonal theme both in the grille and side detailing, while the elegant Buick (bottom) features softer curves. In addition to its fins, the Cadillac (left) is distinguished by an architectural formality of continuous horizontal lines punctuated by verticals in both the grille and side treatment. - SR

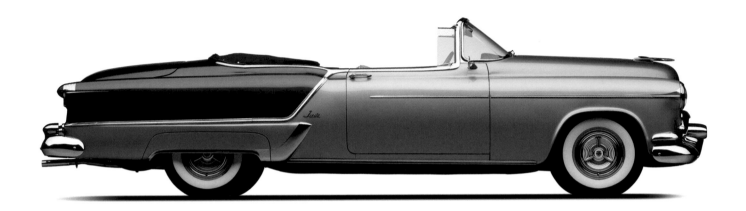

1958 Chevrolet Bel Air Impala Convertible

1957 Cadillac Eldorado Brougham

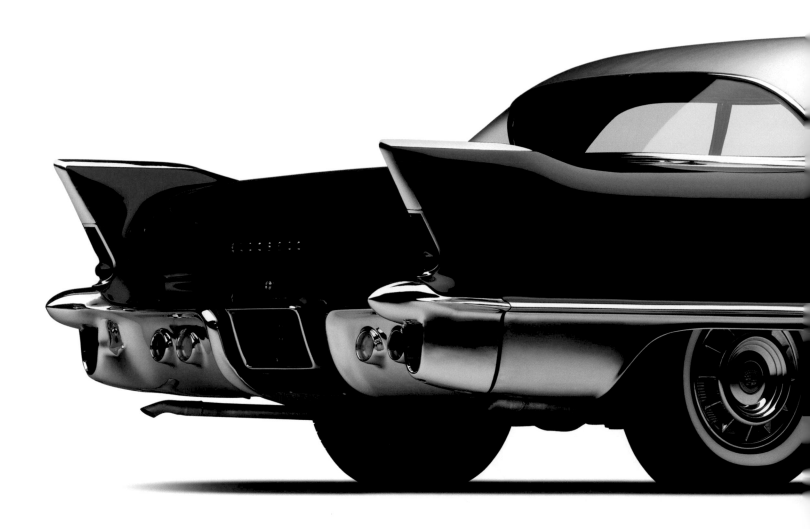

1959 Chevrolet Impala Hardtop, 1959 Cadillac Eldorado Seville Hardtop
1959 Buick Electra Hardtop,

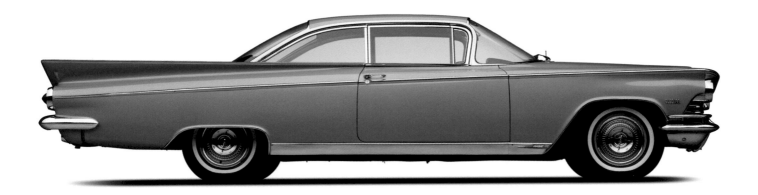

6

No One Even Comes Close: General Motors in the Sixties

By Tony Hossain

The space-age corner office at the General Motors Technical Center in Warren, Michigan, changed hands on December 1, 1958. After 31 years at the helm, Harley Earl gave the candy store keys to his understudy, Wiliam L. Mitchell. Earl was the stuff of legends, and his deft touch gave GM unquestioned design leadership throughout the 1930s, 1940s and 1950s. He loved "futuristic" shapes, and many of his super hits–the 1938 Y-Job, the 1951 LeSabre and the Motorama Firebird turbine cars–reflected his fascination with the jet fighters at nearby Selfridge Air Force base. But times had changed and Earl hadn't. "Beginning in 1958, Romney's Ramblers and the foreign imports were largely responsible for GM's failure to make any appreciable gains in penetration until 1961, when GM countered with its own small cars," reported *Fortune* magazine in 1963.

In 1963, *Fortune* magazine reported:

> At GM today, everyone is striving for what they call "the clean, expensive look." The "bright-work" is vastly less obtrusive than it was several years ago. . . . In the view of Styling's Bill Mitchell, there has been a vast improvement—almost a renaissance—in American taste in recent years; people everywhere are developing a more subtle sense of color, line, and form, and this is reflected in such things as clothing and furniture as well as cars. Today, a good design sells.

Triumphant Triple Play: Sting Ray, Riviera, Grand Prix.

Design historians will always remember 1963 for the three GM cars that sent competing auto stylists scrambling to their "do-over" tables: Corvette Sting Ray, Pontiac Grand Prix and Buick Riviera.

The production '63 Corvette Sting Ray captured the visceral appeal of the original Sting Ray Racer. Offered in traditional convertible or new fastback coupe form, the new 'Vette included peaked front and rear fenders, a sharp character line wrapping around the car, hidden headlamps and a beautiful new interpretation of the Corvette's "dual-cove" instrument panel. The reviews were nothing short of triumphant.

Act II of GM's 1963 triumph, the Buick Riviera, was actually conceived on "spec." In the late 1950s and early 1960s, GM management was tiring of watching the Thunderbirds go by. The four-place 1958-1960 T-Birds were a surprise hit with the prestige set that was rejecting longer, lower, wider Cadillacs, Lincolns and Imperials.

Legend has it that Bill Mitchell had his "epiphany" on a rainy evening in London, as he watched a silver Rolls-Royce glide by. He knew he wanted more than a T-Bird, much more, and directed designer Ned Nickles to "give it the look of a Ferrari/Rolls-Royce." Ensuing sketches became edgy, with a compelling tension that drew the eye. An egg crate grille, with bold vertical parking light covers, suggested the car was meant for Cadillac; Mitchell even named the early clay "LaSalle." The marriage of knife-edged creases and flowing fender lines made the side view equally intriguing, and it was all topped by a formal roofline with elegantly wide C-pillars. Very continental, yet very American, and just about perfect.

Then something unexpected happened: Cadillac didn't want the car. Pontiac was going down another track with the Grand Prix, and Bunkie Knudson, Chevrolet's general manager, thought Chevrolet had too many car lines already. That left Oldsmobile and Buick. Both wanted it. Ed Rollert, Buick's division manager, won the day with a brilliant proposal to name this razor-edged beauty Riviera and promote it as "Buick's bid for a great new international classic." The world's motor press couldn't get enough of this American beauty, and public response was equally enthusiastic.

Pontiac's Grand Prix, was the third head-turner in this vintage season. Worked from a more limited budget, the GP demonstrated the genius of Jack Humbert and the can-do

The restyled full-size 1963 Pontiac was indeed a head-turner, especially in its signature color of Nocturne Blue. Key elements included vertically stacked headlamps and more pronounced, de-chromed rear quarter panels.

This is a Pontiac? This is a Pontiac Grand Prix! '63.

attitude within the Pontiac studios. The starting point was the restyled 1963 full-size Pontiac, a decidedly good place to start. Key elements were vertically stacked headlamps flanking the trademark split grille and more pronounced rear quarter panels, another Pontiac trend that would soon spread industry-wide. The GP took the sheer look to a daring extreme with de-chromed flanks and a concave rear window treatment (shared with the Oldsmobile Starfire). It was a class ride, especially in signature Nocturne Blue with Pontiac's exclusive eight-lug wheel-and-drum assemblies.

GTO Ignites Muscle Car Wars

Enter the 1964s. Full-sizers, Chevrolet through Cadillac, received another round of pleasing facelifts: bigger changes were a year away. Buick's Riviera was largely unchanged, as were Chevrolet's Corvair, Chevy II and Corvette, although the split rear window was history.

The main event consisted of the upsized Buick Special/ Skylark, Oldsmobile F-85/Cutlass and Pontiac Tempest/ LeMans "intermediates," all wearing crisp, clean styling with curved side glass. Sitting atop conventional body-on-frame chassis, the total effect was light-years ahead of the awkward 1961-1963 "BOP-ettes."- (Buick - Oldsmobile - Pontiac). Joining this trio was the Chevrolet Chevelle, available in 300, Malibu and Malibu Super Sport trim levels.

TIME magazine gushed about General Motors, writing:

> Despite the fact that it already sells 52 percent of the nation's autos, giant General Motors keeps itself whipped into a competitive lather—and its largest division is the most competitive of all. Though its sales are already greater than those of the entire Ford Motor Co., Chevrolet has prepared for 1964 a whole new line of intermediate models in an effort to win even more sales. Last week, Chevrolet General Manager Semon ("Bunkie") Knudson showed to the press the auto that is supposed to do the job: the new Chevelle. Impressed by its clean and handsome styling, Detroit's normally undemonstrative auto reporters broke into spontaneous applause.

The cars were mega-hits; GM took charge of the mid-size market and aftershocks abounded: Studebaker closed its South Bend, Indiana, assembly operations in December 1963; Rambler's Classic would never again see 1963-level sales; and Ford's Fairlane was immediately and completely outclassed.

And then, two months after the 1964 model year began, the Tiger roared onto the scene. This special performance option for the handsome LeMans models was spearheaded into production by Pontiac General Manager John Z. DeLorean. The Pontiac chief had the audacity to name this mid-sized Pontiac "GTO," or Gran Turismo Omologato, after a contemporary sports/racing Ferrari. The cognoscenti were outraged.

The GTO packed a big 389 Pontiac V-8 into a middleweight body. Suddenly, 409 Impalas, 427 Galaxies and 421 Catalinas seemed a little too heavy and maybe even a little too slow. *Car & Driver*'s David E. Davis immortalized the GTO almost immediately with a more fiction-than-fact Pontiac GTO vs. Ferrari GTO comparison test.

In a 1975 tribute, Davis vividly recalled the 1964 GTO's appeal. "The message was straight-line speed . . . it felt like losing your virginity, going into combat and tasting your first beer all in about seven seconds."

With production limited to 32,450 units, the GTO was sold out through 1964. The 1965, with its neatly stacked headlamps, hood scoop, wraparound rear lights and distinctive diagonally striped bucket seats, was scooped up by 75,352 enthusiastic buyers.

The man who spearheaded General Motors into the Muscle Car wars was Pontiac General Manager John Z. Delorean (1925-2005). He even had the audacity to name the 1964 LeMans coupe with the special performance option, the "GTO," after the legendary Ferrari sports racing coupe.

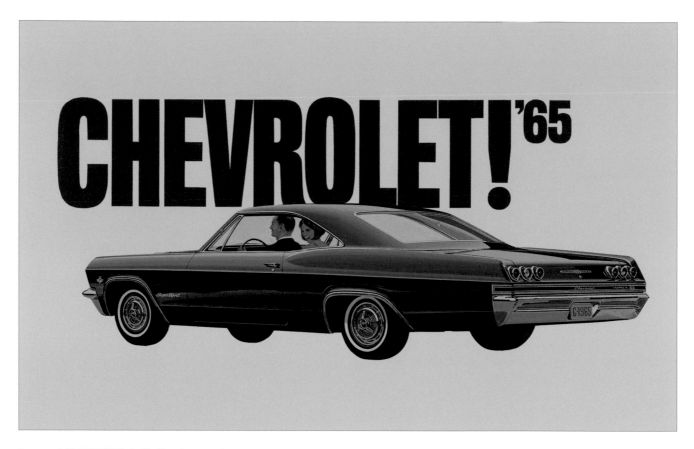

Some call 1965 Bill Mitchell's finest moment. Out of the Chevrolet studios came the exciting new Impala. Everyone at Design Staff knew this one was going to be a mega-hit.

By this time, the Pontiac marketing machine was in overdrive. GTO was the Tiger, Detroit's legendary Woodward Avenue was its turf and, all across the land, the 389-engineded, tri-power Pontiacs were the number one street bullies. The GTO quickly spawned a whole new "muscle-car" category: '66 "Goat"-chasers (including the Chevelle SS 396), the Oldsmobile 4-4-2, the Buick GS400, Ford's Fairlane GT, and "street" versions of the mighty Plymouth/Dodge Hemi cars.

But GTO hype aside, the landscape was starting to look a bit more competitive for GM. After a disastrous 1962, Chrysler was staging a comeback with more conventional styling and a novel 5-year/50,000-mile warranty. Following a truly miserable 1963, Ford announced a game-changer on April 17, 1964; the $2,368 Mustang made the cover of both *TIME* and *Newsweek* in the same week. Mustang fever was about to sweep the land, and from this point forward, the Corvair was a dead duck.

The Sensational 1965s

Some call 1965 Bill Mitchell's finest moment. In a way, it was like 1941. The full-size cars, from Chevrolet to Cadillac, were all sensations. The all-new Corvair was a sweetheart. "We have to go on record and say the Corvair is—in our opinion—the most important new car of the entire crop of '65 models, and the most beautiful car to appear in this country since before World War II," raved *Car and Driver*. Styling had the power at General Motors. And when Mr. Mitchell dictated, "no compromises, just great cars," people listened.

In the Chevrolet studios, excitement surrounded the big new Impala. Set on a new perimeter frame, the big "Chevy" was a breathtaking departure from the angular 1961-1964 full-size autos. The responsibility that goes with designing the biggest-selling car in the industry didn't deter the team, led by Irv Rybicki, from making a statement. Even though there was a load of "Chevrolet" brand character, from a wide horizontal grille to three-to-a-side rear lights, the 1965 was really avant-garde, with a sexy rear-quarter "kick-up," a "floating" knife-edge front bumper and tail lamps that sparkled like expensive jewelry on the gently curving decklid.

Everyone at Design Staff just knew this one was going to be a mega-hit, and it was. Full-size Chevrolet sales hit an all-time high in 1965, with an incredible 1.74 million units. Of these, over one million were Impalas. The record still stands.

Funny thing, the '65 Impala was a last-minute car. That flowing semi-fastback Sport Coupe roofline, which ended up being shared by Pontiac, Oldsmobile and Buick, was a clandestine effort to replace the more Malibu-like roofline Mitchell had already approved.

Long after the 1965s were supposedly "locked in," Irv Rybicki showed the semi-fastback proposal to Mitchell, who immediately fell in love with it. According to Dave Holls, "Mitchell needed GM President Jack Gordon's approval for the last-minute styling changes." Recalled Holls, "Gordon arrived at Design Staff, looked at both clay models, had no appreciation for anything he was seeing and said, 'Ah, Bill it doesn't matter. They both look about the same, don't they?' Mitchell was dumbfounded, blurting out: 'The same? The same! That's like saying Chicago and Paris look the same because they both have rivers running through them!'"

The big Pontiacs were also completely new in 1965. With its sensuous, flowing lines and Coke-bottle sides, the Pontiacs blew away the full-size competition from Ford and Dodge.

The stunning modified fastback was approved for all divisions (except Cadillac) on that day, June 11, 1963.

Retired Chrysler Corporation designer Jeff Godshall recalls the jitters in the Dodge studios:

> The big 1965 Pontiacs were completely new—with sensuous, flowing lines and Coke-bottle body sides that blew away both the Ford and the full-size Dodge. Thus, when it came time to design the all-new "C" series big Dodge for 1967, it seemed that the Dodge studio sketched with one eye on the 1965 Pontiac catalog, where lush renderings shouted from every page, "Top this!"

After those blockbuster 1965s, which shattered all previous sales records across all divisions, there were small, unsettling signs that the best was not yet to come. The 1966 full-size cars were still the mainstays of the corporation, but they seemed to lose, almost imperceptibly, that irresistible edgy combination of youth and elegance that had drawn buyers the year before. Sure, these were still great designs, but across the board the quality was a little uneven, and sales were down, especially at Chevrolet.

Toro. Riv. Eldo. Unrivaled Elegance.

But, for the moment, all eyes were on three absolute works of art. One Oldsmobile. One Buick. One Cadillac. Closely related. Completely different.

The Oldsmobile was, of course, the Toronado. The first U.S. front-driver since the 1937 Cord, the Toro was the absolute sensation of 1966. And if the engineering was astonishing—front wheels powering a 425 cid V8 and a massive full-size chassis—the styling was out-of-this-world.

The first sketch, penned by Oldsmobile stylist David North and nicknamed the "Flame Red Car" because of its stunning color, was pure dream car. Luckily, the big fastback was quickly appropriated by Oldsmobile and went to production in almost record time. Massive wheel openings, a roof that flowed onto the lower body and an outlandishly long hood were the keys to this imposing design. Hidden headlamps, horizontal grille bars and ventilated wheels paid tribute to the Oldsmobile's spiritual ancestor, Gordon Buehrig's 1936 Cord 810. The overall effect: magnificent, masculine and absolutely impossible to ignore.

Over in the Buick studios, lead designer Dave Holls took a quieter approach for the second-generation Riviera. The Buick utilized carryover engineering, including a rear-drive chassis, early 1960s-era "X-frame" and venerable "nailhead" Buick V-8 engine. Atop all this conventional thinking sat one of the most beautifully formed pieces of automotive sculpture to ever leave a GM studio.

Although the '66 Riviera shared glass, cowl and underbody structure with the Toronado and upcoming '67 Eldorado, you'd never know it. Among enthusiasts, the debate of 1966 was, "Which one do you like better—Toro or Riv?" Opinions were many, and there was no wrong answer. Where the Toronado was massive, the Riviera was sensuous. The lines just flowed, from the sculpted hood to the smoothly arched fender lines to a roofline that swept gracefully from rear window to back bumper. The only criticism: to some eyes the car seemed big; it was substantially larger than the elegantly sized 1963-1965 series.

Toronado was *Motor Trend* "Car of the Year." In the showrooms, the Riviera won hands down.

Dealer unrest caused Oldsmobile marketers to quickly retreat from the bold originality of the 1966 and demand a vinyl top option that effectively destroyed the Toro's roofline harmony. Subsequent tinkering through 1970 relentlessly "dumbed-down" the design. Finally, in 1971, Oldsmobile surrendered completely to convention, offering up a timid Eldorado look-alike under the Toronado nameplate. It sold well.

The third member of this trio was Cadillac's 1967 Eldorado. Penned once again by Dave North, this "personal" coupe had prestige buyers on waiting lists. The Eldo boasted another long, classic hood shape and bold egg crate grille with concealed lamps. Razor-edged rear fender lines culminated in vertical taillamps. The look was "Cadillac, all the way," and the '67 Eldo restored the division's reputation for top-drawer merchandise. In Hollywood, the Eldorado replaced the Dual-Ghia as Hollywood's "A-list" car; Sinatra had one, so did Dean Martin.

Camaro and Firebird . . . Finally

It seemed like an eternity but Camaro, Chevy's answer to the Ford Mustang, arrived in the fall of 1966 as a 1967 model. Styling was fully in the GM mold, curvaceous yet tautly formed. Two models were offered, a two-door hardtop and a convertible. Buyers could choose from a variety of option packages, including the RS package with hidden headlamps in a "black-out" grille opening—which added to Camaro style. A high-performance SS 350 package could be ordered with or without the RS package. Within months, a big-block SS 396 option and a special road race-ready Z/28 package were introduced.

Pontiac wanted in on this "pony-chasing" game, but DeLorean's division got a late start. The Firebird, with its own take on the same basic shell, arrived in February 1967. Pontiac engines were fitted, and styling was an attractive take on legendary Pontiac themes: a wraparound bumper/

The 1966 Oldsmobile Toronado was an imposing
design with massive wheel openings, a roof that
flowed onto the lower body and an outlandishly long
hood. It also featured hidden headlamps, horizontal
grille bars and ventilated wheels, making it
impossible to ignore.

1963 Buick Silver Arrow I

Much less an extrovert than previous GM designs, the Silver Arrow I
and its production interpretation, the Riviera, reflect a distinctly
European influence. Combining both the formality of Rolls-Royce
and the sensuality of a Ferrari, it achieves Mitchell's desire. The long,
sharply creased character lines and wide, low grille shape with integrated enclosed headlights emphasize the understated yet dynamic
design. - Stewart Reed

1963 Buick Silver Arrow I, 1963 Buick Riviera

1964 Pontiac GTO

Pontiac's GTO was the original muscle car. With only minor
cues to the performance potential within, the first GTO set
the pattern for later additions of the genre. A clean, simple,
yet well resolved design, the split-grille forms would become
a Pontiac trademark. Fitted with minimal badging, subtleties
belied its power - the informed just knew. - SR

1966 Oldsmobile Toronado, 1967 Cadillac Eldorado

Based on the same front wheel drive E-body platform, these Toronado and Eldorado designs demonstrate two distinct personalities. The blended muscular shape of the sporting Toronado contrasts strongly with the sharp and formal angularity of the Eldorado. Compare the fast C-pillar angle and fuselage body of the Toronado with the formal, vertical roof of the Eldorado, which sits atop a traditional shoulder line. – SR

7

No Time for Design:
New Challenges in the
Post-Oil Crisis Era

By Lawrence R. Gustin

On the morning of the 1972 new-model press preview, touring writers milled around the glass and marble lobby of Buick's world headquarters in Flint, Michigan, taking in the coffee and doughnuts and chatting up General Manager Lee Mays, other executives and each other. They were all killing time, waiting for the PR director, Jerry Rideout, to open the auditorium where the new models would be trotted out. Finally, the moment arrived. And there on the stage, bathed in spotlights, appeared two shiny Buicks—both with their front bumpers caved in. One was a 1971 model, the other a '72. The '71 looked considerably more damaged.

The Cadillac Seville, introduced in May 1975, is cited by some designers as GM's first big exercise in downsizing. This is not exactly true, as it was a new car with no previous models for comparison. But it was 27 inches shorter and 1,000 pounds lighter than the Coupe de Ville, so size was very much a consideration.

The first models to earn the true downsized label were big cars such as the 1977 Chevrolet Caprice and Impala. For 1978, the A-body cars were downsized—Chevrolet Malibu, Buick Century, Pontiac Le Mans, Grand Am and Oldsmobile Cutlass. And for 1979, the E-bodies were shrunk—Cadillac Eldorado, Buick Riviera and Oldsmobile Toronado.

Downsizing affected interiors perhaps even more than exteriors. "When you downsize a vehicle, you limit the crush space available to compress in an impact," explained Tatseos.

> Impact zones for knee, thorax and head move into the passenger space, and more exotic materials to manage compression are required. Money that might have been spent to improve the quality of visible interior materials is instead spent where the customer can't see it, behind the instrument panel or inside the doors. A lot of times as studio chief, I was fighting to keep the quality of interiors ... almost everyone wanted to downgrade something—cheaper fabrics, plastics, etc. It was rare to have a chance to upgrade to a better quality material.

In the middle of all this, there was a seismic shift in management at the top of GM Design. Bill Mitchell, the second Design vice president in GM's history, a talented, energetic leader often described as a "wild man," retired in 1977. The legendary Harley Earl (Design chief 1927-1958) had selected Mitchell as his successor, and for the most part, his years as Design boss (1958-1977) were successful.

Mitchell had a passion for great design, and he instilled that ardor in his subordinates. The man was undeniably a character. He worked hard and played hard. The first dozen years of Mitchell's time at the top were made-to-order for him—it was a freewheeling time for design, and Mitchell's team turned out success after success. In the late 1970s, designer Jerry Hirshberg noted, "Mitchell ran the place as a movie director—like Cecil B. DeMille. But to his credit, he sometimes liked a little controversy. Too often we are intimidated by all the regulations."

Mitchell and his predecessor were both strong leaders. When six foot four Harley Earl came aboard to create a separate GM design operation in 1927, he fought a number of early skirmishes to earn a free rein—and it certainly helped to have the strong support of legendary GM President Alfred P. Sloan, Jr.

And Mitchell was certainly combative. In the 1970s, the late, great GM designer Ned Nickles said, "Harley Earl was one of the finest people to work for—very demanding but very appreciative. He couldn't design himself, but he knew what he wanted. Earl would give you credit in front of anyone. Mitchell had an art background and was a car nut. He wanted to take all the credit. He was forceful but at times insulting."

Kady remembers an argument between Mitchell and Buick General Manager George Elges over plans for the 1978 Riviera.

> Elges, who wanted a less expressive design after getting rid of the boattail [a controversial previous design], had already argued with Mitchell. Elges wanted to see what the '78 Olds Toronado and Cadillac Eldorado would look like. Mitchell told me to make sure Elges didn't get into those studios. Then later, in my office, they almost came to a fist fight. Mitchell could be crude. He was calling Elges names. Elges was upset but he didn't back down. He still wanted to see the Olds and Cadillac studios, and finally Mitchell took him there. At one point, he told Elges, 'Nobody likes you—not even Kady.' I didn't like him saying that. Later Mitchell began berating Elges about his taste in the clothes he was wearing. When Elges asked me later if what Mitchell said was true, that I didn't like him, I told him Mitchell didn't speak for me.

Contentious though he was, Mitchell was not immune to the forces that so heavily impacted design. The downsized cars created during his final years were particularly hated by Dave Holls, one of Mitchell's chief lieutenants, though Holls did concede that Ford and Chrysler were having terrible times, too. When it was time for Mitchell to retire, it turned

1979 Cadillac Seville

Representing a necessary adaptation to the increasing
bumper and dimensional regulations of the time, the 1979
and 1985 Seville designs seek to create a handsome, stately
impression that reconciles the overall form of the car to the
large, squared-off bumper shapes. The result is unavoidably
rectilinear and static, particularly as shown on the earlier
model. – SR

1985 Cadillac Seville

1979 Cadillac Seville, 1985 Cadillac Seville

In profile, the '85 Eldorado's attempt at dynamism is most evident. Quite effective in its execution, the design's steeply angled rear window and "bustleback" form provide a welcome relief from the strict verticality of the '79 model. This interpretation of the classic Rolls-Royce 'trunk' form integration was controversial. – SR

8

The Art of Colour at General Motors:
The Use of Color in Design

By Jeffrey I. Godshall

In 1954, Harley Earl, GM's pioneering and legendary Vice President of Styling, succinctly stated his overall design philosophy: "My primary purpose in car styling . . . has been to lengthen and lower the American automobile, at times in reality and always . . . in appearance. Why? Because my sense of proportion tells me that oblongs are more attractive than squares." Invited in 1927 by GM President Alfred P. Sloan, Jr. to set up the Art and Colour Section, a group that would advise GM's multiple divisions on automotive appearance, Earl and his talented staff always tried to achieve distinction through the artful use of color. Earl's initial effort for GM, the breakthrough 1927 LaSalle, which he designed before establishing Art and Colour, employed darker-colored fenders, hood and cowl contrasted against a lighter-colored body to create a smart "European" effect.

Return of the Two-Tone

Ironically, just as the goal of unifying the automobile exterior through the use of a single color was achieved, two-tone finishes became popular. Initially, this was accomplished "on the cheap," with some two-color Pontiacs appearing with contrasting-color fenders merely bolted on. This jumbled look was soon replaced by applying the contrasting color (usually a lighter variant of the lower body) to the upper body, roof and upper door frames. This disrupted Fisher Body's paint operations due to the extra time and masking involved. Nonetheless, two-tones became increasingly popular with buyers. The division line between the upper and lower body colors created another horizontal element which made the cars look lower and longer in tune with Earl's preference of rectangles over squares.

With the Depression finally behind them as the 1940s debuted, Americans became more optimistic. Reflecting this change in the nation's psyche, GM's car colors became more adventurous, offering customers a cornucopia of exuberant choices—grassy greens, orangey reds, cheery yellows, milky creams, burnished golds and elegant dark, medium and light grays, in both metallic and straight shades. One classic color combination used on early 1940s Buick convertibles daringly mated a deep blue exterior with a lipstick-red leather interior, accented with Dante Red metallic wheels. The effect was both dramatic and brashly confident.

GM stylists took advantage of color to dramatize the look of their glamorous new fastbacks that debuted on 1941's Pontiacs, Oldsmobiles, Buicks and Cadillacs (Chevrolet joined the club in 1942). Offered in two- and four-door iterations, the new streamliners were a risky departure for GM. In the late 1930s, when given a choice of fastback or notchback body styles, buyers had overwhelmingly chosen the notchback variants with their larger trunks. Yet the new, recast GM fastbacks proved quite popular. To accent their new streamlining, the roof, upper door frames and sloping deck lid were often painted a light color. The effect was evocative of a young girl, her face to the wind, her long, blond hair streaming back behind her. In 1941, Earl and his stylists were at the top of their game, offering customers an unbeatable combination of attractive styling, creative use of color and jewelry-like bright accents.

1941 AUTO STYLE BALLOT

Which of the new styles would you "VOTE FOR" as being:-

"BEST LOOKING" ↓   "LEAST ATTRACTIVE" ↓

Check GM Products

☑ □ — ⓐ B U I C K — □ ☑
□ — ⓑ C A D I L L A C — □
□ — ⓒ C H E V R O L E T — □
□ — ⓓ C H R Y S L E R — □
□ — ⓔ C R O S L E Y — □
□ — ⓕ D E S O T O — □

□ — ⓖ D O D G E — □
□ — ⓗ F O R D — □
□ — ⓘ H U D S O N — □
□ — ⓙ L I N C O L N - Z E P H Y R — □
□ — ⓚ M E R C U R Y — □
□ — ⓛ N A S H — □

□ — ⓜ O L D S M O B I L E — □
□ — ⓝ P A C K A R D — □
□ — ⓞ P L Y M O U T H — □
□ — ⓟ P O N T I A C — □
□ — ⓡ S T U D E B A K E R — □
□ — ⓢ W I L L Y S "A M E R I C A R" — □

Make of car now owned? ....

Year model? ....

This "1941 Auto Style Ballot" was an early attempt at a market survey mailed out by General Motors Customer Research. Although the results of this vote are not available, it is hard to believe that the attractive styling, creative use of color, and bright accents of GM's products could have been beaten.

Opposite - These 1941 Buicks are an example of how the streamlining of GM's popular new fastbacks was accented with color. By painting the roof, upper doorframes and sloping deck lid a lighter color, the flowing lines are emphasized.

MODEL 61—*Six-passenger four-door sedan*

MODEL 66-S—*Six-passenger sedanet, with full-width rear seat*

featured Polar White bodies with twin blue racing stripes. Beginning in 1973, Pontiac began offering seriously extroverted Firebird customers an elaborately colored "firebird" decal (nicknamed the "screaming chicken") that covered most of the hood; only a car as boldly styled as the Firebird could have pulled it off. Pontiac's pioneering mid-size muscle car, the legendary GTO, boasted U.S. Royal "Tiger-paws" red line tires with a narrow red stripe replacing the customary whitewalls. During 1966-1967, GTO buyers could even opt for red fender liners as well, shaped to tuck inside the distinctive oval wheelhouses and offering a truly unique color accent.

In 1968, Oldsmobile offered the first in a long run of Hurst-equipped versions of its Cutlass 4-4-2; but, as the years wore on, the car's usual gold and white paint scheme became a caricature of itself. Even the normally staid Buick let its hair down on such cars as the 1970 GSX, in "catch me if you can" bright Saturn Yellow with a blacked-out hood and full-length body side racing stripe that lifted up and over the rear deck spoiler.

During this Beatles era of supercharged creativity, the guys in the Pontiac Studio found yet another way to use color to harmonize the overall look of the car—the Endura bumper. Developed in conjunction with the engineers at GM's Inland Division, the urethane front bumper was molded around a metal armature, then painted body color. Debuting on the all-new '68 GTO, the split-grille, color-keyed Endura face enabled GM designers to make the bumper appear as an integral part of the car body, rather than an add-on chrome appendage. The Endura nosepiece was the forerunner of the color-keyed fascias used universally on cars today.

Identity Through Color

Understanding that color is the easiest way to add newness, on many occasions, GM has used color to establish a car's "image." The white and blue Firebird Trans Am already cited is one example. On Chevrolet's 1955 Cameo Carrier pickup, the white body color was chosen to emphasize the visual unity of the cab and the new flush pickup box. The first 2,000 or so of Pontiac's funky 1969 GTO Judges were each painted a vivid, orangey Carousel Red, after which other colors were available. Likewise, the first few months' production of Cadillac's 1976 compact luxury sedan, the Seville, were all cloaked in upscale silver with matching silver vinyl roofs and leather interiors. When the plant began building the comely Sevilles in other colors, it was like introducing the car all over again. In pristine black, dressed with wire wheel covers and a vibrant orange pinstripe, the Seville was absolutely stunning.

Though GM cars have been built in a wide variety of colors, there are some cars and colors that have become inexorably linked in our collective memory: colors such as Shadow Gray/Coral on '55 Chevys, the mustardy Laurel Green/Crocus Yellow combo offered in 1956 and the pinkish Dusk Pearl/Imperial Ivory in 1957. Pontiac's stunning '63 Grand Prix will always be remembered in that deep, dark blue (Nocturne) that dramatized its de-chromed exterior. Likewise, the purplish Burgundy on the 1966 front-drive Olds Toronado—could there have been any other appropriate color? And who can forget the light violet, metallic Evening Orchid used on the '65 Chevrolet Impala, or the Verdoro Green ("Bell Telephone green") on the first Pontiac Firebirds?

Ironically, the designers' success in using color to unify the shape of the automobile has resulted in fewer choices for today's customers. Due to increased manufacturing complexities, the current prevalence of body-color front and rear fascias, door handles and side view mirrors has meant that buyers are limited to 9 to 12 exterior colors instead of the 15 to 20 selections offered when these parts were a "neutral" chrome. The use of water-based paints (robotically applied in "clean rooms") and the mandating of environmentally-responsible pigments has also eroded our choices. Similarly, interior selections today seem to be limited to warm or cool gray, in part because popular SUVs require more interior trim parts than cars with untrimmed trunks. The increased complexity is offset by reducing color choices. Compare this with the 1970 Pontiac GTO, with its rainbow palette of 21 exterior and 6 interior colors.

This trend may be changing. The successful new Chevrolet Malibu boasts a smart, two-tone black and tan interior, while Buick's Enclave offers an elegant cocoa-colored exterior and interior combination. Still, the next time you see a Bolero Red '67 Camaro SS ragtop with matching red interior, top down on a sunny day, take time to savor its saturating, soul-satisfying redness. Color-wise, you're not likely to see such eye-popping glories again.

styled to stay new...

with FLYING COLORS!

Give your fancy free rein! Oldsmobile lets you practically color-customize your car with striking effect! From the boldly dramatic to the sophisticated, every Oldsmobile bears an exclusive and unmistakable stamp of the future . . . to keep you far ahead in the style parade.

This 1955 Oldsmobile Sales brochure shows the seemingly infinite color possibilities offered to customers. This allowed buyers to "keep far ahead in the style parade." Or at least until the 1956 models arrived!

1940 LaSalle Series 52 Convertible

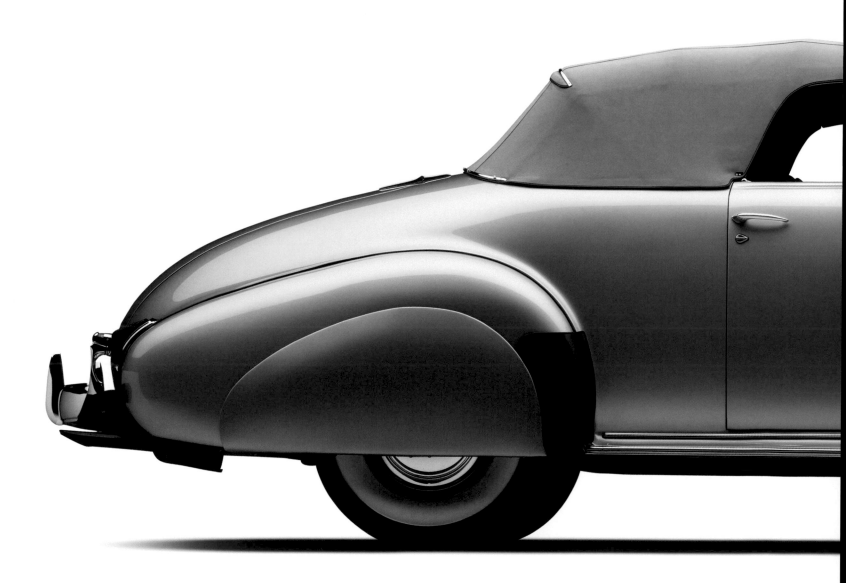

Nobody could have predicted the immense effect the bright colors of the Harley Earl era would have on the future of car design. The platinum metallic on this LaSalle serves to amplify and accentuate its gentle form. - SR

1950 Oldsmobile Holiday Deluxe Coupe, 1956 Pontiac Chieftain Coupe,
1956 Chevrolet Two-Ten Sport Coupe

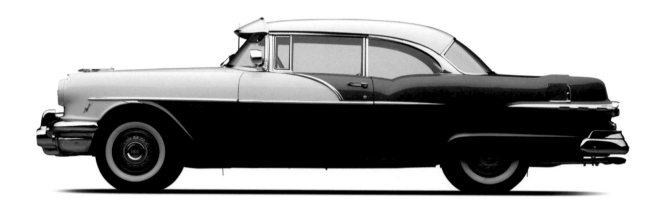

With the diverse color palettes, bodywork dripping with stainless
and chrome accents of the vibrant 1950s, the cars above represent
flamboyant interpretations of Harley Earl's desire to "lengthen
and lower" the automobile. In each case shown, the color
combinations and compositions serve to visually lower the car
by breaking up the mass. The streaks of stainless along the sides
guide the eye from the front to the rear of the vehicle, length is
accentuated and the car is kept in perpetual motion. - SR

1956 Pontiac Chieftain Coupe

1957 Chevrolet Bel Air Convertible

1957 Chevrolet Nomad

In any color combination, the 1957 Chevrolet is a design icon, but the fusion of the shape of the car with the GM's contemporary color palette represents a seminal event for the era. The jet-age inspired stainless spears and finely textured rear fender inserts mimic the shoulder profile, stretching out the already dramatic length of the body side. Whether in soft metallics, vibrant primaries or subtle pastels, the design is undeniably beautiful. - SR

1970 Chevrolet Chevelle SS 396

Muscle cars such as the Chevelle, GTO Judge and Olds 4-4-2 presented their credentials proudly. During their reign, they wore stripes, evocative badges, and colors that screamed performance. Unlike previous uses of color and subtle trim to highlight design's form, the intention here is to intimidate and display inner qualities of power and acceleration . . . perfectly accented by a pair of black burnout marks. – SR

1971 Pontiac GTO Judge, 1971 Oldsmobile Cutlass 4-4-2

9

Camaro:
The Evolving Design Process

By Ed Welburn

I've been interested in developing a new Camaro concept vehicle for a number of years—one of my personal cars is a 1969 Camaro SS. Early in 2005, two things came together to move that idea ahead. First, work on GM's next generation of global rear-wheel drive vehicles was progressing. That new architecture was ideal for the creation of cars with dramatic proportions. Second, Bob Lutz and I saw a trend toward cars that built on the heritage of their brands, and I proposed that no vehicle would exemplify this better than a Camaro-"Let's do a Camaro concept." GM's Warren Advanced Studio, led by Bob Boniface, was given the assignment, and my 1969 Camaro was made available for inspiration and design reviews. I wanted them to be inspired by my car, but I also wanted them to beat it! I wanted a very contemporary design.

called Studio X. This is the same secret studio where Bill Mitchell developed numerous very special projects.

Managed properly, I feel that a "friendly" competition between design teams always benefits the design process. The head-to-head competition between the two studios made each design stronger. When questioned about the competition, Bob Boniface was sure that "each team worked on making their car the best it could be."

"The Camaro concept program was a microcosm of how product development should work," Boniface added. "Once the Advanced studio and engineers had the package and proportions right, the Production studio could go faster with more confidence."

As work progressed, each team traveled across the Warren campus to keep an eye on the other's work. "We had recon missions going back and forth. This is the way things should work in a car company," declared Boniface.

Show Time

The decision had been made on April 5, 2005, to push ahead with a concept car, code-named CZ6, for the North American International Auto Show in Detroit in early January 2006. The pressure from the tight schedule for finalizing the design and building a running vehicle was compounded by a sense of the importance the Camaro had to millions of fans. These fans included the designers: Bob Boniface, whose first car was a second-generation Camaro; Tom Peters, who also owns a 1969 Camaro- and me.

Throughout, there was a constant tension between a desire to honor the heritage of the first-generation Camaro, and a recognition that the new car had to compete with the best rear-drive sports coupes from around the world.

Even though there were no production plans for the car, everyone involved hoped the car would be built and felt that the final concept should be very close to what customers would be able to buy.

"This wasn't just a show car. We didn't want to just tease people with a show car. It had to be producible," explained Tom Peters.

While the exterior design drew inspiration from the first-generation Camaro, most specifically the 1969 model, the interior was more modern in execution. There was no single Camaro interior considered iconic, so the interior design team at the Warren Advanced Studio combined select Camaro cues into a thoroughly modern interior. Boniface made the point that "the execution, the fit and finish, could only have come from the modern era."

As the summer of 2005 ended, we held a "bake-off" on the Design Center patio with both full-size clay models flanking my 1969 Camaro SS. I settled on the Production Studio's design. But it's fair to say that the friendly rivalry and the intense sharing of ideas back and forth between the studios meant that the final car was produced by both studio teams.

"The passion won out. The car people won. The car guys in design and engineering demanded that this car happen," said Boniface, "and that it be a truly modern interpretation of a Camaro. We couldn't allow the idea to die on the vine. And that says a lot about the enthusiasm and passion here at GM."

The public unveiling of the Camaro concept at the North American International Auto Show in Detroit was one of the most thrilling experiences of my career. Thousands of people attended. There was a marching band and a parade of significant first-generation Camaros, including the black and gold Smokey Yunick Camaro, the legendary Sunoco Camaro, Tom Peters's 427 1969 Camaro and my yellow 1969 Camaro SS. Lloyd Reuss, chief engineer of the original Camaro (and GM president from 1990 until 1993) was there, and the owner of the race-winning Sunoco Camaros, Roger Penske, spoke from high on a tower. It was great theater.

When Bob Lutz drove the Camaro Concept onto the stage, grown men and women had tears of joy in their eyes. It was an emotional experience for Camaro enthusiasts and a source of pride for all GM employees.

Opposite Top - Here, both Ed Welburn and Bob Lutz examine one of the competing clay models.

Opposite Bottom - The public reveal of the 2009 Camaro concept took place at the North American International Auto Show on January 9, 2006.

1969 Chevrolet Camaro Z/28

2009 Chevrolet Camaro

The new Camaro includes all the necessary and memorable theme elements for a Z/28 in a thoroughly contemporary way. The new front is lower and more ground-related for aerodynamic reasons yet still carries the aggressive high front grille graphics. - Stewart Reed

The new Camaro is much more wheel-oriented and powerful looking than the early design. It is 3-dimensionally sculpted, yet pure Camaro. – SR

In 2002, Lutz eliminated the archaic "brand character" design studio approach. In its place, five new design units were established for body-on-frame vehicles, unibody vehicles, advanced vehicles, character and interiors, and design center engineering each under an executive director. Now, when initial designs are completed as scale models, design executives and top management conduct "bake-offs" to narrow the field before submitting the winners to consumer clinics.

In 2003, Lutz appointed Ed Welburn (who'd been in charge of body-on-frame designs) to succeed the retiring Design VP Wayne Cherry. With Lutz's encouragement, Cherry began the modern GM Design renaissance with high-profile concept cars such as the Cadillac Sixteen, Chevy SSR and Pontiac Solstice.

The tide has turned. Auto show goers once again flock to GM stands with the excitement and anticipation of Motorama attendees over half a century ago.

Ed Welburn, who carries the title of General Motors Vice President, Global Design, is only the sixth GM Design leader in the company's 100 year history. The man responsible for the record-setting Oldsmobile Aerotech racer of 1987, he occupies Harley Earl's old office at the GM Design Center in Warren, Michigan. The soft-spoken Welburn credits his passion for cars back to when his father took him to GM's Philadelphia Motorama, and he was rendered speechless by the Cadillac Cyclone showcar.

Welburn clearly understands the importance of each division's individual brand character as key factors of design and engineering. And he's a student of GM history, an important quality when you're responsible for reinterpreting and updating brand heritages.

The GM concept car pattern that began in the 1950s has been reinvigorated. Since 1999, GM Design has been responsible for more than 50 concept cars for its divisions. Chevrolet, Pontiac and Buick can point to a rich history of design studies that led to memorable new models. Cadillac, however, has been totally resurrected, proof that truly great design can lead the way to desirable production cars.

Chevrolet - Value, With Flair

In the mid-1950s, Chevrolet's constantly evolving styling, highlighted by virtually all-new models every year and energetic V-8 performance, kept the division high on the sales charts. But as the century closed, Chevrolet had lost much of its distinctiveness.

Ed Welburn and Bob Lutz unveil the new Cadillac CTS, which _Motor Trend_ magazine named "Car of the Year" for 2008.

**The 1959 Cadillac Cyclone show car that inspired
Ed Welburn's passion for cars.**

As if to recapture that '50s flair, Chevrolet's 1999 Nomad was an intriguing, two-door concept wagon that prompted memories of the production 1955-1957 Nomads so enduringly popular with hot-rodders and customizers. Built on a fourth-generation Camaro/Firebird platform, with a fold-down rear deck and the flashy trim spears of its namesake, the Nomad's prominent fender flares, Corvette-like grille and aggressive stance could have prompted a lasting Chevrolet design direction. However when the rear-drive F-body platform was discontinued, any hope for production ended.

In 2002, again exploring links with its past, Chevy debuted a Bel Air Convertible concept at the Detroit Auto Show. "This is not just another convertible," said Wayne Cherry. "The Bel Air is about embracing the essence of those mid-'50s Chevies, in a contemporary way." The concept convertible's in-line turbocharged 5-cylinder engine was also an engineering dead end, at least for Chevrolet passenger cars. Alas, the sprightly Bel Air had almost no influence on series production Impalas, Malibus and Monte Carlos of the next few years.

Again at Detroit, in 2004, Chevrolet debuted another Nomad concept car. The born-again Nomad, designed by Briton Simon Cox, was a miniature design study of its predecessor. A true four-seater, it was powered by the Pontiac Solstice's optional twin-cam, turbocharged inline four-cylinder engine. This Nomad was both dynamically capable and practical. An abbreviated version of the classic early 1950s Corvette grille and stylized covered headlamps rounded out an attractive concept that was an immediate hit, even though production was unlikely. The Nomad showed that there were intriguing Chevy design cues just waiting to be revived.

The M3X Concept two-door sedan (2004) was a Daewoo Matiz update that evidenced how Chevrolet would interpret a microcar. This theme would again be explored in 2007 with the Beat, Trax and Groove concepts at the New York Auto Show. Whether cute city-cars like these could be profitably produced and sold in America was still conjecture. Chevrolet's production 2007 Aveo compact, which displayed many signature bowtie styling elements, albeit in scaled-down form, was imported from South Korea.

Chevrolet debuted its 53X SUV in Geneva in 2005; the sleek lines presaged its production Equinox model and hinted, with a trimmer bowtie grille bar and more rounded styling themes, of more distinctive Chevrolets to come. The division enticed Brian Nesbitt (the lead designer of the popular PT Cruiser) from Chrysler, and the result was the dashing little HHR, a retro-styled, upright, compact station wagon, inspired by the 1949 Chevrolet Suburban. First shown in Los Angeles in 2005, the HHR was subsequently launched as a production model in 2006.

One study with great potential was the 2007 Chevrolet Volt Concept, the first application of GM's vaunted E-flex platform. A two-door sedan, roughly the size of a Chevy Cobalt, the Volt's razor-edged styling was reminiscent of the edgy, futuristic and now, very well-accepted design theme popularized by Cadillac. But there were Chevrolet cues, as well.

Short overhangs, significant fender flares, including tapered reveals that swept rearward from the front wheel arches, a dramatically low roofline windows that dropped below the beltline, a built-in rear spoiler, prominent side "shoulders" and large wheels located smartly to the car's corners, all made the Volt appear more like a European sport compact coupe than an economical runabout. The trim

panels just below the A-pillars opened to expose this car's practical 110-volt charging plugs. In a neat touch, the door handles were hidden in the door trim chrome strips.

Powered by a turbocharged, 1.0-liter, 71 hp, three-cylinder internal combustion engine, with no connection to the car's wheels, this internal combustion power plant instead drives a 53kW generator that, in turn, charges the Volt's lithium ion battery pack. The engine's purpose is simply to charge the battery, stopping and starting as needed. The 136kW battery pack is the power source for a 161 hp (120kW) electric motor that drives the front wheels.

With a range of just 40 miles on the battery pack alone, the Volt hardly seems practical. But with a full 12-gallon fuel load, the Volt can travel 640 miles. Flex fuel-capable, the engine can run on gasoline or any ethanol combination from E10 up to E85. GM engineers estimated that, for a commuter who drove 40 miles per day, the Volt could save some 500 gallons of fuel annually. The engine/generator combination permits 70 mph cruising and charges the battery in 30 minutes of operation.

The Volt was intended to be the first electric car that would permit drivers to enjoy flexible travel. The obstacle, as this is written, is the Volt's battery. To date, no affordable battery exists that would permit 100,000 miles of operation, but GM engineers are confident such a battery could be developed. If its technical challenges can be overcome, it could spawn a host of spin-offs, saving fuel without sacrificing either style or lifestyle. It's likely that some of the Volt's styling cues will be reflected in future Chevrolets. And, if GM can work out the technology challenges, the Volt will surely inspire other manufacturers.

Most recently, the Chevrolet Camaro coupe concept (2006) and convertible (2007) reprised and updated the iconic '69 Camaro. Thanks to a stunning design that builds on storied history, and to popular acclaim, a production 2009 Camaro was assured (see Chapter 9, "Camaro: The Evolving Design Process"), and it's sure to bring excitement and attention to Chevrolet.

Chevrolet found its groove with the Opel-based Malibu in 2008. At last, much of the distinctiveness of popular Chevy design is present. The Malibu's crisp styling, well thought-out appointments, value for money and smart performance helped it win "North American Car of the Year" honors and a place on *Car and Driver*'s coveted "10 Best" list. Along with the 200+ mph Corvette ZR1 prototype, Chevrolet is pursuing the looks and performance that made it "The Hot One" for years.

Pontiac: Performance and a Great Deal More

During the John Z. DeLorean era back in the 1960's, Pontiac was transformed from a mainstream, rather stodgy brand into a high-performance and styling tour de force. A wide-track stance, split-grilles, thin pillars, crisp clean lines and plenty of V-8 punch were Pontiac hallmarks. But, in the years that followed, component rationalization and corporate timidity diluted Pontiac's distinctiveness.

GM touted Pontiac as its performance division, and the heritage of the original 1964 Tempest GTO remains an enduring muscle car memory. On the eve of the new millennium, Pontiac presented two concepts. One was the odd-looking Aztek crossover, which was doomed to ignominy. The other, the Holden-based GTO, eventually failed because it lacked the distinctive looks of the car's original namesake or of the 1999 GTO concept. Although its road-going performance was memorable, sales lagged and the production GTO was discontinued after a few years.

Conversely, the 2002 Pontiac Solstice Coupe and Roadster Concepts, the first GM show cars influenced by Bob Lutz, pointed the way to an exciting production Solstice roadster in 2006. That car subsequently spawned the Saturn Sky two-seater in 2007 and, in 2008, a revised Solstice coupe concept. Tightly wrapped, with signature Pontiac twin grilles, close-cropped overhangs, tall wheels, rear-drive adapted from GM's Kappa platform, and packing a hopped-up

Eco-tech 4-cylinder engine, the Solstice became a true Miata-fighter.

Pontiac offered a G6 Concept car in 2003 that mirrored the Solstice roadster's grille and aggressive rake but in four-door guise. While the cool-looking show car featured smooth lines, 20-inch wheels, a supercharged V-6 and high performance brakes, the road-going production car evolved two years later with fewer of these features. That said, a distinctive Pontiac "look" was becoming evident: cat's-eye headlamps, that noticeable forward tilt, wheels-to-the-corners, tightly wrapped bodywork and a driver-oriented cockpit all signaled "sport sedan" in keeping with the brand's performance heritage. Pontiac's 2006 production G6 reflected the show car's styling.

At the 2008 New York Auto Show, Pontiac displayed a rear-drive G8 GXP sedan prototype, slated for 2009, with a Corvette-derived 6.2-liter, 402 bhp V-8 and a flashy G8 Sport truck, both sourced in Australia. While the big news was Pontiac's return to V-8 engines, both concepts displayed dual-port grilles, side vents, lower front splitter fascias, 19-inch wheels and slick interiors. Some have termed the G8 GXP "an American BMW from Down Under." Once again, Pontiac is serious about performance.

Pontiac teased attendees at the 2008 Melbourne, Australia, Motor Show with a G8 GXP Coupe Concept. GM insiders cautioned "Don't call it a GTO or a Firebird." Although it resembles a hardtop, like the 2009 Camaro, if produced, it will have a subtle B-pillar and will compete with the Dodge Challenger. Pontiac styling has evolved clearly; there's no mistaking a Pontiac for any other GM car today, just as it was in the 1960s when the Widetracks and GTOs ruled America's roads.

Pontiac offered a four-door G6 concept in 2003, that shows a distinctive brand look is once again emerging. Many of its styling cues made it into the 2006 production G6.

Buick: Recapturing the Magic

Next to Cadillac, Buick styling has arguably been the most creatively consistent of any GM division. Beginning with the elegant four-door hardtop convertible Cielo show car of 1999, Buick has re-initiated many historic styling cues, from pronounced vertical grille bars reminiscent of the famous pre-World War II Y-Job, to functional triple portholes and a dramatically dipped beltline emulating popular 1940s and 1950s side-spears.

While the Cielo did not directly relate to any production model, the LaCrosse sedan that followed in 1999 was a direct precursor to modern Buick themes. The LaCrosse, resplendent in a "deep wine" hue, could be converted into a stylish pickup, and it was guaranteed to intrigue show-goers. Its doors opened a full 90 degrees; the roof could be completely opened, along with the windows. A pillarless design contributed to a feeling of openness and permitted more flexible seating. Once again, the wide grille, exaggerated portholes and beltline dip all underscored that this was a Buick.

The racy Buick Blackhawk, also from 1999, was a 2+2 hardtop/convertible that resembled custom rods of the 1940s and 1950s. While the metallic, dark maroon Blackhawk evoked a favorable response from the rod and custom crowd, it was purely an exercise to celebrate Buick's performance heritage.

In 2001, Buick presented the snappy Bengal roadster, a two-tone Asigiri (silver-blue metallic) two-seater with a wheelbase nearly as long as the LeSabre's. However, thanks to the Bengal's abbreviated overhangs, it was some 25-inches shorter. A small door located behind the driver's door facilitated access to a hidden storage compartment behind the seats. Apparently, Buick had no plans to build it. Appearing with spokesman Tiger Woods, the Bengal was designed to attract younger buyers.

Buick showed the Centieme in 2003, an elegant crossover proposal that led directly to the curvaceous 2007 Enclave. A stylish head-turner in a compromised category where most competitors resemble shrunken minivans, it's easy to see why Buick had so many advance orders for the very successful Enclave. The acceptance of this model, and its success in attracting new buyers augured well.

With the vintage "Riv" in mind, Buick's Shanghai studio produced a stunning concept in 2007. Clearly a proposal for a modern Riviera, it deftly used all the now-familiar Buick visual identifiers. And after a 45-year hiatus, at the 2008 Bejing Motor Show, Buick revealed a signature hardtop that revived the Invicta nameplate. Fittingly, Buick remains one the most popular marques in China. This stunning showcar, with its signature waterfall grille, evocative side-spear and futuristic portholes, more than hinted at the direction of Buicks to come.

The spectacular Cadillac Evoq roadster was named the "Best Concept Car" by *AutoWeek* at the 1999 North American International Auto Show. This was the first car to preview GM's 21st century design direction. The Evoq clearly demonstrated Cadillac's "Art and Science Design Strategy," which was a fresh design language that would soon make its way into the production models.

Cadillac: Playing all the Angles

Cadillac had long been GM's image-enhancing luxury brand, but after enduring repeated import onslaughts from Mercedes-Benz, BMW, Jaguar and Lexus, GM's premier division was poised for a renaissance. Its major objective was to retain core Cadillac customers while appealing to younger buyers.

Through a series of incorrect decisions, Cadillac had diluted much of its strong visual identity, and its public perception had plummeted. Cadillac General Manager John Smith asked GM Design chief Wayne Cherry to take Cadillac's iconic, fantastically be-finned 1959 model and "fast-forward" it 40 years. Through sketches and proposals that excited members of the GM strategy board, a fresh, new design direction evolved.

Iconic Cadillac styling elements—vertical headlights and taillights, egg crate grilles, rakish and angular panels—led the way. There were risks involved, but it was riskier not to take a chance. The new vision for Cadillac's renaissance was expressed as "Art and Science." It took time before production models would mirror this bold new look, so the challenge fell on concept cars to point the way, engage the public, accustom buyers to new direction, and eventually translate into salable production models.

It started with one spectacular roadster that was the first major concept car to preview GM's 21st century design direction. The Cadillac Evoq roadster bowed in at the 1999 North American International Auto Show in Detroit and was acclaimed "Best Concept Car" by *AutoWeek*.

Designed by Kip Wasenko, this edgy little two-seater, with its sharply V-shaped grille, razor-edged reveals, ultra-clean lines and built-in rake, clearly demonstrated Cadillac's "Art and Science Design Strategy," a "fresh design language" that would soon be reflected in production cars.

The genius of the Evoq was the way it recaptured Cadillac styling nuances without descending into the temporarily attractive but short-lived retro look. The Evoq fairly shouted "futuristic," "bold," "high tech" and, as Bob Lutz would later say, it was a "gotta have!" car.

Perhaps anticipating the future increasing cost of fuel, the Corvette-based Evoq was fitted with a 4.2-liter, 405 bhp, supercharged Northstar V-8. The Evoq's folding metal hard-top previewed contemporary trends, as did its Michelin Pax run-flat tires on tall 19-inch front and 21-inch rear wheels and neon rear lighting.

From a color perspective, the slender, razor-edged Evoq was finished in metallic pearlescent pewter, a variable-appearing shade Cadillac called Argentanium, which accentuated the roadster's crisp, sharp lines. The Evoq's interior, comprised of contrasting tan and charcoal leather, was replete with matte finish aluminum trim and discrete gray plastic rocker switches.

Cadillac optimistically promised interested parties that the Evoq roadster would be available in 2002. The division made good its promise the following year with the Corvette-based 2003 XLR.

At Geneva in 2000, Cadillac debuted the Imaj, the division's first all-wheel-drive car. The big, bold, four-door sedan, with an aluminum spaceframe chassis, was styled in GM's Birmingham, England, studio by Simon Cox. Contemporary auto writers referred to the Imaj as a "sport limousine" or a "four-place, ultra-grand tourer." The exercise purported to show how the Evoq roadster's long-nose, short-deck classic sports car proportions and strong edges would translate into what *Car and Driver*'s Frank Markus called "an unconventional, short-nose, long-cabin, micro-deck shape." He noted that the Imaj's 16.7-foot (5.1-meter) length was ideally suited to the spaces in European parking garages.

Crafted with a look in Cadillac's historic rearview mirror, the aptly named Imaj featured twin brushed aluminum roof rails and functional air extractors in the V-shaped hood. The suicide rear doors were a tribute to Cadillac's limited-production 1957 Eldorado Brougham four-door hardtop. The Imaj's curved roof was covered with electrochromic panels capable of changing from clear glass to transparent white or completely opaque, simply by varying the voltage across their surfaces.

The Imaj was powered by an updated 425 bhp version of the four-cam 4.2-liter Cadillac Northstar V-8 mated to a five-speed automatic transmission. Performance for the 0-to-60 sprint was estimated at 6.1 seconds, despite an estimated curb weight of 4,100 pounds.

Meanwhile, Cadillac unveiled its 2002 Cien concept roadster with a DOHC, 750 bhp Northstar V-12, Displacement-on-Demand technology (so it could run as a fuel-saving six) and

trapezoidal air inlets to cool twin front-mounted radiators. Functional side air intakes and exhaust vents opened only when needed.

Another Simon Cox design, the one-off Cien resembled an F-22 Raptor stealth fighter. Its sharp-edged panels and rigid chassis were formed of lightweight, very stiff carbon fiber. Scissor-style doors pivoted upward at the base of the forward A-pillars. Once again, the use of a silvery hue and the refined angularity of the Cien's shape evoked the look of production Cadillacs to come.

Although a true production car, the Escalade sport utility attracted the kind of attention often drawn by concepts. The Escalade was an overnight hit with many older Cadillac buyers and, more importantly, with urban youth, professional athletes and other celebrities. "Gonna get me a 'Slade," was the cry, and these sporty trucks attracted many new people to Cadillac showrooms.

The most dramatic GM concept car of the early 21st century was the stupendous Cadillac Sixteen. Cadillac was under intense pressure to respond to the new Bugatti Veyron, BMW's revival of Rolls-Royce and Mercedes-Benz's luxurious Maybach. At the North American Auto Show, GM's luxury division surprised everyone with a head-turning two and one-half ton behemoth. The Sixteen evoked both the company's original V-16 cars of the 1930s and the 1931 Bugatti Type 41 Royale, thanks to its audacious size and sheer magnificence, not to mention a colossal, 1000 bhp, 13.6-liter V-16 powerplant with Displacement-on-Demand. GM's advanced design team for the Sixteen was led by the company's styling chief, Wayne Cherry.

The Sixteen's enormous 24-inch wheels, with 265/40R24 tires, relegated well into the corners, anchoring a perfectly proportioned, ultra-long wheelbase that would've done credit to a Duesenberg. Overall the car was nearly 19 feet long, but its trim waistline and low-mounted aluminum side-spears made it look smaller. The Sixteen's lengthy hood folded open on both sides, reminiscent of a 1930s-era classic.

Resplendent in dark tones with crisp Cadillac styling cues, the Sixteen helped hammer home what had become a consistent message: no matter how large or small this car may be, make no mistake this is a Cadillac.

The Sixteen was a big hit wherever it was shown. Far from being a dead end in a chain of Cadillac styling studies, it underscored the crisp, bold direction that has become Cadillac's 21st century trademark.

The production XLR delivered many of the Evoq concept car's advances. Its exterior styling was largely unchanged from the show car. And while it was hardly an overnight sales hit, the XLR's styling prepared admirers for the edgy

revolution that would become a Cadillac hallmark. The Escalade, the CTS, and later the SRX began to make sense. This was the new look of Cadillac. Aided by an in-your-face advertising and marketing approach, suddenly Cadillac was cool again.

The XLR had tough competition, including the Mercedes-Benz SL500, the Lexus SC430 and the Jaguar XK8. The XLR roadster didn't try to compete in a styling sense; it didn't have to. It was an American statement, pure and simple. The Corvette-based chassis needed no apologies. The eucalyptus wood trim was unique, as was the instrumentation, designed by renowned jeweler (and vintage GM car fan) Nicola Bulgari.

According to chief engineer Dave Hill, "The use of composites (not aluminum as first planned) facilitated its crisp character lines and flat surfaces." The result was a 320 bhp, Northstar V-8 powered two-seater that was 400 pounds lighter than a 500SL.

The XLR may not have been a huge seller but, like its inspiration, the Evoq, it deserves a great deal of credit for Cadillac's success today.

At Detroit- in January 2008, Cadillac again intrigued North American International Auto Show-goers. The razor-edged coupe design on display employed styling elements from the popular CTS and CTS-V sedans and blended them with all-new sculpted bodywork, beginning with the Coupe's trim, two-seater cabin and running through its neatly nipped rear fenders.

Ed Welburn noted, "We did not create it as the result of sifting through reams of market data, nor is its shape trimmed to suit the input collected at a consumer clinic. It is emotion on four wheels and the very essence of what defines Cadillac today."

The CTS Coupe's "fast-rake styling" shared the production sedan's wheelbase, but the Coupe was two inches lower and two inches shorter. The bodywork shape was hand-sculpted in the studio, permitting a fender design that flared outward around the four wheels. Signature design cues included angular elements designed to suggest "the look of a meticulously cut diamond." The rear fenders were beveled in keeping with the diamond theme. They became part of a horizontal plane that ran from the leading edge of the tail-lamps and merged into the roof.

According to John Manoogian II, Cadillac's director of exterior design, "The CTS Coupe uses these [cut diamond] elements, along with nods to classic Cadillac cues like vertical lighting, to acknowledge brand heritage without resorting to nostalgia."

While based on the production sedan, the CTS Coupe shares only the four-door's instrument panel, console, headlamps, front fenders and grille. Unique elements include: hardtop styling without a B-pillar, a production CTS windshield raked rearward at a faster angle, chromed aluminum 20-inch front wheels and 21-inch rear wheels, a sculpted lower front fascia with brake-cooling vents, XLR-type hidden door handles and unique front fender vent.

In keeping with a sporty 2+2 specification, the Coupe uses the sedan's 304 hp Direct Injection V-6, along with a six-speed manual transmission. The Coupe concept has been designed for a new 2.9 liter turbo-diesel engine being developed for GM's international markets. Adapted for the CTS, the diesel will deliver about 250 bhp horsepower and a whopping 406 lbs/ft. of torque.

AutoWeek magazine named the Coupe the "Best Concept" of the 2008 North American International Auto Show, the same honor bestowed on the Evoq ten years earlier. Now, great cars were expected from GM's luxury division. Although exact dates were not announced, Cadillac insiders hinted a production version would be available in 2009. Cadillac's advertising and promotion have expertly supported styling and engineering. A 2008 ad teases buyers: "In today's luxury game, the real question is, when you turn your car on, does it return the favor?"

From the 1999 Evoq to the 2008 Cadillac CTS Coupe Concept, with superb support from GM engineering and marketing, General Motors designers have consistently created a range of distinctive, futuristic vehicles-in just one decade-that appeal to a widening swath of appreciative audiences. The Cadillac renaissance is a fine example of how great design can resurrect a brand. Cadillac has regained all the visual impact and presence the brand commanded in its heyday.

This much is clear: As the 21st century unwinds, the legacy of Harley Earl and Bill Mitchell remains in very good hands.

Opposite Top - The Cadillac Sixteen was the most dramatic GM concept car of the early 21st century. The design team was led by the company's styling chief, Wayne Cherry (seen with the car in the newly restored lobby at the Design Center).

Opposite Bottom - The Cadillac CTS Coupe debuted at the North American International Auto Show in January 2008. Like the Evoq ten years earlier, it was also named "Best Concept" of the show.

2000 Chevrolet SSR Concept

2000 Cadillac Imaj Concept

The Imaj was imposing and confident, even with very compact
dimensions. Simon Cox's response to the classic Cadillac
elements included disciplined, stretched surfaces, sharp
edges and stacked lamps. The front view is pure Cadillac with
a modern take on the classic "egg crate" grille. The rear view
emphasizes the trademark vertical taillights, connecting
them with sheer, knife-edged surfaces. – Stewart Reed

2000 Cadillac Imaj Concept

2002 Cadillac Cien Concept

**The Cien proved the strong Cadillac form language could be
effectively applied to an exotic mid-engine aspirational car.
The strong, wedging shoulder concludes with a bold, very
powerful rear and showcases the V-12 engine, giving the cabin
a very compact appearance. – SR**

2002 Cadillac Cien Concept

2003 Cadillac Sixteen Concept

The Cadillac Sixteen symbolizes the reinvention of the Cadillac brand. The extremely long hood proportions set the cabin back on the chassis giving a sporting feel to an unbelievably large car. Notably restrained, with cleanly executed surfaces and remarkably limited brightwork, the design is none the less opulent and dramatic. Subtle detailing is proportioned so as to draw further attention to the car's commanding presence. With the characteristic large grille and vertically stacked headlamps, the identity is unmistakable, yet the result is forward-looking. – SR

2003 Cadillac Sixteen Concept

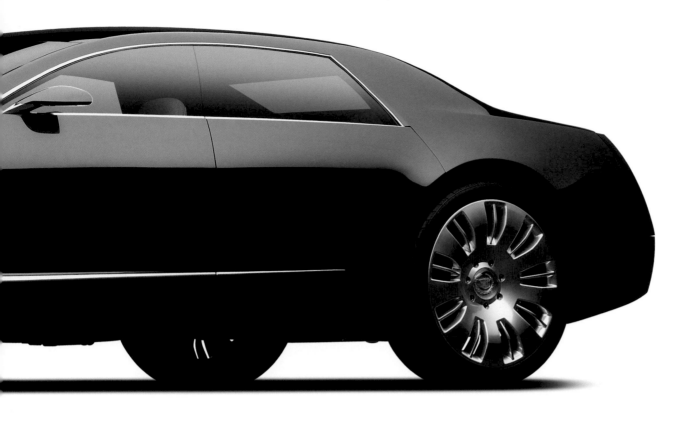

2007 Chevrolet Volt Concept

With extremely short front and rear overhangs, the Volt's
design theme seeks to match the boldness of its underlying
mechanicals. The high shoulder line gives the greenhouse a
short, chopped appearance, while the integrated transparent
element provides an uncompromised view outside. The rear
fenders appear to protrude beyond the centerline, revealing
a compact bustleback, emphasizing the smart packaging and
limiting the overall size and visual weight. – SR

2008 Cadillac CTS

The dominance of the "Art and Science" angularity in the XLR has given way to a blending of classically beautiful, muscular side surfaces with knife-edged intersections in the CTS. The strict horizontality of the front end graphic has morphed into a more imposing grille in size and shape, while the stacked head lights have remained a key feature. Indeed, the application of the design themes from concept to production has proven the pliability of the character traits and relevance to all categories of Cadillac vehicles. – SR

2008 Cadillac XLR

2008 Cadillac XLR

Reinvigorating the sporting nature of the Pontiac brand, the
Solstice represents a return to the classically derived profile.
The design places the emphasis on curvaceous surface development
and compact dimensions. It is a uniquely American take on the small,
sporting roadster and demonstrates this character with a rolling
beltline, trim headrest fairings- and large, wide-eyed headlamps.
Particularly nice is the small recess that trails the Pontiac badge,
giving the impression of forward motion. - SR

Afterword
By Richard S. Adatto With Shana Hinds

General Motors has been a crossroads for automotive ideas and innovations since its inception in 1908. William Durant, the company's founder, was an avid purchaser of competing technologies, and his passion set GM on the path that would eventually make it a model of international business. In those early days, GM's designs were born of a meeting of American minds. As the company absorbed various coachbuilders, GM's aesthetic resources expanded exponentially. Later, the company sought ideas from all over the world by observing the latest models at auto salons in Paris, Berlin and London, and by importing European designers or stationing American designers overseas. Today, the world of automotive styling has become a very small place indeed. With design studios in nine foreign countries, GM is positioned to bring internationally inspired styling to new heights.

During the first half of the 20th century, stylists from the United States and Europe continually influenced each other in their pursuit of the perfect automotive shape. GM's role in this international exchange was, in part, the result of Harley Earl's interest in European designs. Initially hired by Cadillac President Larry Fisher to create the LaSalle, Earl later became the first director of The Art and Colour Section. Earl soon assembled a team of talented designers, and the resultant models were unprecedented successes. The 1933 Cadillac V-16, the 1938 Buick Y-Job and the 1953 Corvette are just a few examples of the inspiration taken from the coachbuilders of Italy, Germany and France. In turn, the many trendsetting models created by Earl and his team had a profound impact on their foreign counterparts. As former GM Senior Creative Director George Camp put it, "Design doesn't evolve in a vacuum, and designers are conscious of the efforts of their peers worldwide." Earl's designs are proof positive of this assertion.

The GM Styling Section (as it was renamed in 1937) remained under the direction of Harley Earl until his retire-ment in 1958. He was succeeded by Bill Mitchell, who shifted the department's focus toward overall style and shape but retained and nurtured GM's international relationships. The design of the Chevrolet Corvair, the first car produced under the new reign, inspired the designs of several high profile European manufacturers. Even as General Motors continued to draw inspiration from abroad, it simultaneously provided innovations to a world that demanded continual improvement.

In the late 1960s, GM started to lose touch with the demands of the world market. Concentrating on large, spacious, fuel-thirsty vehicles, the company began to lose the entry-level American market to foreign imports. Then in 1973, the international gas crisis struck and economy cars soared in popularity. When the United States Government reacted to the situation by setting fuel economy standards and imposing new regulations, GM's current line of big cars just couldn't compete. With domestic profits at an all-time low, the company was forced to downsize its models and retrench.

Although GM's sales were faltering in the United States, the company, fortunately, had profitable foreign divisions. In the 1920s, GM purchased Vauxhall Motors in England (1925) and Opel in Germany (1929). In 1983, the design programs for both subsidiaries were combined under the leadership of Wayne Cherry. Cherry was a talented designer who, in 1962, after impressing the GM Styling department, had been sent to England to further his craft. By 1987, the designs of the Vauhall/Opel Technical Development Center had become Europe's top selling mod-els. The European operation was a major and much-needed profit center for GM during the late 1980s and 1990s. When Cherry returned to the United States in 1991 and became Vice President of GM Design, he brought with him the ideas and innovations that made cars successful on a global level.

Also helpful during GM's dark days was its Australian

subsidiary, GM Holden. Purchased by GM in 1931, Holden is to Australia what Chevrolet is to the United States—its cars are everywhere. Australian designer Richard Ferlazzo once claimed, "Nearly everyone in Australia had a connection to one (a Holden) at one time or another—owned one, rode in one, or was conceived in one." GM Holden helped maintain GM's international presence during this difficult period.

GM's global presence was originally established to give the company a broader market base and encourage an international approach to design and technology. It is fortunate that the powers at General Motors possessed such foresight. With the support of its foreign divisions, GM was able to survive the years of the gas crisis and actively recognize the importance of international influences. It was this recognition that led General Motors to re-establish and expand its global connections in the final decade of the twentieth century.

In the late 1990s, GM took a momentous step. Taking its cue from the successful GM design centers in the United Kingdom, Australia and Germany, it began establishing design studios in other parts of the world. Sweden, Japan, China, Korea, Brazil and, most recently, India have all become homes to General Motors' designers in recent years. Such on the spot offices perfectly position GM to take advantage of emerging markets, such as the one in South Asia. Additionally, each location takes inspiration from the trends and styles indigenous to its area, and these influences are all funneled back to the Design Center in Detroit. As Ed Welburn explained in a 2007 interview, ". . . it was like GM was four different car companies. The design studios in individual regions were not linked. Now we have one global design studio that I lead."

In 2001, Bob Lutz rejoined GM as Vice Chairman of Global Product Development. He knew that, "In terms of competitive challenge, it's truly become a global industry," and he personally renewed the focus on design to meet the demands of the time. Within a few years the company was ready to reap the benefits of its efforts. The Cadillac CTS, unveiled in 2002 for the 2003 model year, is credited with rejuvenating the Cadillac brand and possibly saving it from extinction. With edgy styling—GM calls it "Art and Science"—the car succeeded in capturing an international buyer base with a modern take on streamlined styling.

When Wayne Cherry retired in 2004, Ed Welburn was appointed Vice President of Global Design, a newly minted post reflective of GM's evolving international position. Welburn, like Cherry, has rotated through GM's German operations and has the necessary awareness of global market demands. The designs produced thus far under his leadership, such as the 2008 CTS (named *Motor Trend* "Car of the Year"), bode well for GM's future. Welburn knows that the company is headed in the right direction and avows "What we're building today, I believe in." And judging from the CTS's international reception, the world believes in it, too.

GM was an important force during the first forty years of automotive styling, and a large number of the company's successes can be attributed to the incorporation of international design elements. The 1927 LaSalle, the 1933 V-16 Cadillac Aerodynamic Coupe, the 1953 Corvette: all these models were clearly inspired by European designs and details. General Motors made automotive styling a legitimate and necessary aspect of a profitable business. By adopting the very best design motifs and influences the world had to offer, GM made its Art and Colour Section the global authority on design and styling. That the company has now regained its former focus is cause for rejoicing. That this revival was accomplished by a renewal of international influence is historic.

Author/Contributor Biographies

Phil Patton

The author of many books on design and culture, Phil Patton writes about automobile design for *The New York Times* and other publications. He has served as consultant for museum exhibitions at the Phoenix Art Museum and the Museum of Modern Art in New York. He has taught at the Columbia Graduate School of Journalism and School of Visual Arts. Patton has also appeared as a commentator on several television programs aired on PBS and the History Channel.

Terry V. Boyce

Terry Boyce started writing an automotive column for his hometown Kansas newspaper in 1965. Over the past four decades, his byline has appeared in many car magazines. He is a former editor of *Old Cars Weekly* and has authored several car books. Recently retired from a 20-year career as Director of Product Information for Chevrolet's ad agency, Terry lives near Detroit and is now focusing full-time on automotive history projects.

Michael Lamm

Automotive historian, writer and publisher Mike Lamm was born in London, England, and grew up in South Texas. He fell in love with cars at an early age and, after college, worked in New York as editor of a VW magazine. In 1962, he became managing editor of *Motor Trend*. In 1970, Mike founded *Special-Interest Autos* and, eight years later, began publishing books under the Lamm-Morada banner.

Jerry Burton

Jerry Burton is the founding editor of *Corvette Quarterly* and a creative director on the Chevrolet account at Campbell-Ewald. He also serves as the executive editor of *Hagerty's* magazine published for Hagerty Insurance. A former *AutoWeek* motorsports editor, Burton is the author of *Zora Arkus-Duntov, the Legend Behind Corvette*, as well as the just-released *Corvette: America's Sports Car, Yesterday, Today and Tomorrow*.

Tracy Powell

With a Journalism degree from Indiana University, Tracy Powell's writing and reporting has appeared in numerous newspapers and magazines with worldwide audiences. Residing in Charlestown, Indiana, he is a member of the Society of Professional Journalists and the Society of Automotive Historians, and is managing editor at both *Automobile Quarterly and Auto Events Magazine.*

Tony Hossain

Enthusiast, Chevrolet collector and writer Tony Hossain worked on the Chevrolet account at Campbell-Ewald Advertising, writing Camaro, Impala and Corvette brochures, auto-show materials and websites from 1985 through 2008. Before joining CE, Tony was editor of *Old Cars Weekly* and Associate Editor of *Collectible Automobile Magazine*. Tony is on the Vehicle Selection Committee for the prestigious Meadow Brook Concours d'Elegance, held every August in Rochester, Michigan.

Lawrence R. Gustin

Retired from Buick public relations, automotive journalist and historian Larry Gustin has authored: *Billy Durant: Creator of General Motors* and *David Buick's Marvelous Motor Car: The man and the automobile that launched General Motors* in 2006. He also co-authored, with Terry B. Dunham, *The Buick: A Complete History*. In addition to writing scores of automotive articles, he helped create the Sloan Museum's Buick Gallery and Research Center in 1998 and directed Buick's centennial activities.

Jeffrey I. Godshall

Jeff Godshall worked in the product design office of Chrysler LLC for 45 years before retiring in 2007 as a Senior Design Manager. He worked on exterior and interior projects, from 1960s Dodge muscle cars to the Chrysler PT Cruiser. A long-time member of the Society of Automotive Historians, he has authored numerous articles on automotive history from his personal perspective as a professional automotive designer and long-time student of the automobile.

Edward T. Welburn, Jr.

Ed Welburn was appointed General Motors' Vice President-Global Design on March 1, 2005, and is responsible for design of all GM products worldwide. He began his career with General Motors in 1972, working in various production and advanced studios in the United States and Germany. Originally from Philadelphia, he has a bachelor's degree from the College of Fine Arts at Howard University.

Ken Gross

Automotive writer, historian and collector Ken Gross is the former director of the Petersen Automotive Musem and consults for the Saratoga Automobile Museum and Atlanta's High Museum of Art. He contributes to *Playboy, Hemispheres, The Robb Report, The Rodder's Journal, Street Rodder* and *Hot Rod Magazine*. His books include *Milestone Hot Rods, The Illustrated BMW Buyer's Guide*, and *Ferrari 250GT SWB*. His latest book, *Art of the Hot Rod*, will be published in the Fall of 2008.

Richard S. Adatto

Richard Adatto is one of the world's leading experts on pre-war French aerodynamic cars. He sits on the Advisory Board of the Pebble Beach Concours d'Elegance, an event at which he has judged for more than 20 years. He is the author of *Delahaye Styling and Design, Delage Styling and Design* and *From Passion to Perfection*, and he is the co-author of *Curves of Steel*. His articles have appeared in major magazines. Mr. Adatto lives in Seattle, Washington.

Shana Hinds

Shana Hinds is a freelance copy editor. She is the editor of *Sustainably Sushi*, to be published by North Atlantic Books in early 2009; she has edited pieces for the *Seattle Daily Journal of Commerce*; and is working on several other full-length pieces for national publishers. She lives in Seattle, Washington.

Stewart Reed

Stewart Reed is a well-known automobile designer who consults with major automakers around the world. An Art Center Alumnus, he began his career winning design awards from General Motors. He is currently the Chair of the Transportation Department of Art Center College of Design in Pasadena, California.

Jonathan A. Stein

Editor Jonathan Stein is a veteran of *Automobile Quarterly* and Bentley Publishers. Now Director of Publications for Hagerty Insurance and Associate Publisher of *Hagerty's* magazine, he has authored *British Sports Cars in America, The Performing Art of the American Automobile*, co-authored *Curves of Steel*, and edited many other automotive books. His articles have appeared in a variety of automotive publications. A frequent concours judge, he and his family live in Reading, Pennsylvania.

Michael Furman

Photographer Michael Furman is internationally known for his insightful studio portraits of the world's greatest cars. He has produced a number of titles in recent years including those for the Ralph Lauren exhibit at the Museum of Fine Arts, Boston and the Curves of Steel exhibit at the Phoenix Museum of Art in 2007. His work can be seen regularly in *Classic And Sports Car, Auto Aficionado, Automobiles Classiques* and *Automobile Magazine*.

Bibliography

Adatto, Richard. From Passion to Perfection: *The Story of French Streamlined Styling 1930-1939*. Paris: SPE Barthélémy, 2002.

Automobile Quarterly editors. *GM: The First 75 Years of Transportation Products*. Automobile Quarterly Editors. Princeton: Automobile Quarterly Publications, 1983.

Bayley, Stephen. *Harley Earl and the Dream Machine*. New York: Alfred A. Knopf, 1993.

Beasley, Norman. *Knudsen: A Biography*. New York: McGraw-Hill Book Co., Inc., 1947.

Bellu, Serge. *500 Fantastic Cars: A Century of the World's Concept Cars*. Paris: Editions Solar, 2002.

Berghoff, Bruce. *The Gm Motorama: Dream Cars of the Fifties*. Osceola, WI: MBI Publishing, 1995.

Boyce, Terry V. "The Ultra-Modern Mode: 1940-41 GM C-Bodies." *Automobile Quarterly* 19, no. 3 (July–September 1981).

Buehrig, Gordon M., and William S. Jackson. Rolling Sculpture: *A Designer and His Work*. Newfoundland, NJ: Haessner Publishing, 1975.

Casteele, Dennis. *The Cars of Oldsmobile*. Sarasota, FL: Crestline Publishing Co., 1981.

Clarke, Sally H. "Managing Design: The Art and Colour Section At General Motors, 1927-1941." *Journal of Design History* (1999).

Clarke, Sally H. *Trust and Power: Consumers, the Modern Corporation, and the Making of the United States Automobile Market*. New York: Cambridge University Press, 2007.

Cray, Ed. *Chrome Colossus: General Motors and Its Times*. New York: McGraw-Hill, 1980.

Dredge, Richard. *Concept Cars: Designing for the Future*. San Diego: Thunder Bay Press, 2004.

Ellis, Jim. *Billboards to Buicks: Advertising–As I Lived It*. New York: Abelard-Schuman, 1963.

Frumkin, Michael J., and Phil Hall. *American Dream Cars: 60 Years of the Best Concept Vehicles*. Iola, WI: Krause Publications, 2002.

Furman, Michael. *Motorcars of the Classic Era*. New York: Harry N. Abrams, 2003.

Furman, Michael. *Automobiles of the Chrome Age: 1946-1960*. New York: Harry N. Abrams, 2004.

General Motors Styling Section. *Modes and Motors*. Detroit: General Motors, 1937.

Gunnell; John. *75 Years of Pontiac Oakland*. Sarasota, FL: Crestline Publishing Co., 1982.

Gustin, Lawrence R., and Terry B. Dunham. *The Buick: A Complete History*. 6th ed. Kutztown, PA: Automobile Quarterly Publications, 2002.

Hendry, Maurice D. *Cadillac, Standard of the World: The Complete History*. With updates by Dave Holls. 4th ed.

Princeton: Automobile Quarterly Publications, 1994.
Holstrom, Darwin. *Camaro Forty Years*. St. Paul, MN:
MBI Publishing, 2007.

Janicki, Edward. *Cars Detroit Never Built*. New York:
Sterling Publishing, Inc., 1990.

Kimes, Beverly Rae. "Part One: 1911-1954." *Chevrolet:
A History From 1911*. Princeton: Automobile Quarterly
Publications, 1984.

Kimes, Beverly Rae. *The Standard Catalog of American
Cars: 1805-1942*. Iola, WI: Krause Publications, 1985.

Kuhn, Arthur J. *GM Passes Ford, 1918-1938: Designing
the General Motors Performance-Control System*.
The Pennsylvania State University, 1986.

Lamm, Michael and Strother MacMinn. "A History of
American Automobile Design, 1930-1950." *Detroit Style:
Automotive Form 1925-1950*. Detroit: The Detroit Institute
of Arts, 1985.

Lamm, Michael and Dave Holls. *A Century of Automotive
Style: 100 Years of American Car Design*. Stockton, CA:
Lamm-Morada Publishing Co., 1997.

May, George S. "Harley Jefferson Earl." *The Encyclopedia
of American Business History and Biography*, 1989.

McCall, Walter M. P. *80 Years of Cadillac LaSalle*. Sarasota,
FL: Crestline Publishing Co., 1982.

Newcomb, James. "Depression Auto Styling." *Winterthur
Portfolio*. Vol. 35, No. 1. University of Chicago Press, 2000.

Powell, Tracy. *General Motors Styling 1927-1958: Genesis of
the World's Largest Design Studios*. Charlestown, IN:
Powell House Publishing, 2007.

Schild, James J. *Fleetwood: The Company and the
Coachcraft*; Columbia, IL: The Auto Review, 2001.

Schneider, Roy A. Cadillacs of the Forties. Temple City, CA:
Automobile Heritage Publishing Co., 1976.

Schneider, Roy A. *Sixteen Cylinder Motorcars*. Temple City,
CA: Automobile Heritage Publishing Co., 1974.

Sharf, Virginia. *Taking the Wheel: Women and the Coming
of the Motor Age*. New York: Free Press, 1991.

Sloan, Jr., Alfred P. *My Years with General Motors*.
New York: Doubleday, Inc., 1963.

Stein, Jonathan A. *The Performing Art of the American
Automobile*. Philadelphia, PA: Coachbuilt Press, 2006.

Temple, David W. *GM's Motorama: The Glamorous Show
Cars of a Cultural Phenomenon*. Osceola, WI:
MBI Publishing, 2006.

Unattributed. "General Motors II: Chevrolet." *Fortune*,
January 1940.

Van Gelderen, Ron and Matt Larson. *LaSalle: Cadillac's
Companion Car*. Paducah, KY: Turner Publishing Co., 2000.

Various authors. *Power in Motion: The Automotive Design
Career of Bill Mitchell*. Dearborn, MI: Henry Ford Museum
& Greenfield Village, 1989.

Acknowledgements

The Art and Colour of General Motors is an invaluable work chronicling the evolution of GM's design heritage, a tale that must not be lost to the sands of time. Coachbuilt Press is grateful to the talented team whose hard work and expertise brought this history to the printed page. Without them, it would have been impossible to tell this very important story.

A special thank you to Bob Lutz, Ed Welburn and Teckla Rhoads, who understood the value of GM's design legacy and made GM's vast historical resources available; Greg Wallace and his staff at the GM Heritage Center; the GM Archives, led by archivist Jennifer Knightstep Lesniak; the writing team, led by editor Jonathan A. Stein with copy editors Merrill Furman and Shana Hinds; and Phil Neff, Project Manager, who coordinated the shooting schedule, historical captions and research.

The book's design was by Kerry Polite, Polite Design, with assistance from Susan Skarsgard of General Motors and Mary Dunham and David Philips of Michael Furman Studio.

The Art and Colour of General Motors was printed by Master Printer Bob Tursack of Brilliant Graphics, Exton, Pennsylvania. Bob's printing talents perfectly complement the text and imagery. Further technical assistance came from John Fetter and Bill Pulver.

The publishers also wish to thank Shelly Lesse, Kristen Schuerlein, Robby Rothfeld, Don Stewart, Jim Liao, Pete Adams, Andrew Gibbs, Mitchell and Eleanor Furman, and Marc Furman for their constant support.

The authors would like to acknowledge and thank everyone who helped with their research:

Michael Lamm would like to extend thanks to Don Layton and Al Batts of the Futurliner Restoration Project, *Special Interest Autos Magazine*, J.P. Vettraino of *AutoWeek* magazine, Beverly Rae Kimes, and interviews with William L. Mitchell, Charles M. Jordan and Tom Christianson of General Motors Corp.

Larry Gustin would like to thank former Design Chief Chuck Jordan as well as GM designers Bill Porter, Wayne Kady, Paul Tatseos, Jerry Palmer, George Camp, Clark Lincoln and Dennis Little. Mr. Gustin is also grateful to additional source materials, which came from much earlier (1970s) interviews with former Design Chief Bill Mitchell and designers Ned Nickles and Jerry Hirshberg, as well as assistance from historian Michael Lamm. Also invaluable was research gathered from Gustin's more than 40 years covering the auto industry for newspapers, magazines and books and participating in the business as Buick assistant PR director.

Ed Welburn would like to thank Mike Albano and Ken Gross, while Ken Gross is grateful to Ed Welburn and Wayne Cherry. Phil Neff would like to thank Jennifer Knightstep Lesniak, Pat Chappell, Bob and Grace Gluck and Jim Jordan for their assistance in research and fact checking.

Particular thanks is owed to the individuals, museums and collections that made their General Motors cars available to us for inclusion in this title:

Tim Brickel, courtesy of County Corvette
Nicola Bulgari
Wayne Dascher
Gene and Marlene Epstein
Jay Hammond
The Hendricks Collection at the Gateway Auto Museum
The General Motors Heritage Collection
The Kerbeck Collection
Tom and Carol Kidd
Richard and Gene Laird
Mark Lankford
The LeMay Museum
Bob Lutz
Steve Maconi
David Markel
David Mayo
The Nethercutt Collection
Jeff Pergl
Steve Piaccio
Joe Puleo
Paul and Lois Reedy
Joseph Santaniello
Russell Schempp
The Sloan Museum
Bill and Stacey Smart
D.M. Spaulding
Richard Stanley

Michael Furman and crew photographing the
1956 Buick Centurian in the historic Design Dome,
Warren, Michigan. February 2008

Photography Credits

The imagery in *The Art and Colour of General Motors* is a mixture of historical and contemporary work. The early photographs, documents, advertising and artwork were provided by a number of important archives and private collections. The General Motors Archive, with the assistance of Larry Kinsell and lead archivist Jennifer Knightstep Lesniak, provided the images that form the basis of our historical content. Many of these photographs have not been seen by the public for decades. Other unique and insightful images came from the archives of Richard Adatto, Terry V. Boyce, The Simeone Foundation Museum and The Free Library of Philadelphia's Automotive Collections. We thank everyone for their contributions.

The contemporary studio photographs were taken at a number of locations around the United States, including the GM Heritage Center and the historically significant Design Dome at the GM Technical Center. Greg Wallace and his staff at the Heritage Center and Andrea Gillett, Dale Jacobson and Marci Marentette at the Design Dome made these extensive photo shoots possible. Peter Mullin made facilities available in Oxnard, California, as did John Burzichelli in Paulsboro, New Jersey. Their support enabled us to more completely capture GM's design heritage.

The photography crew included Phil Neff, Dave March, Ken Burgess, Jim Mital, Shawn Brackbill, Chris Koontz and Esteban Granados. The image manipulation and postproduction was performed by the staff at Michael Furman Studio, including Senior Graphic Artist David Phillips and Graphics Specialist Mary Dunham.

All photographs were captured digitally with the Phase-One P45 Digital Back on a Hasselblad H camera, with strobe lighting by Broncolor. All postproduction work involved Mac computers running CaptureOne, Photoshop and InDesign software.

Michael Furman

Published by
Coachbuilt Press
Philadelphia, Pennsylvania, USA
www.CoachbuiltPress.com

ISBN 9780977980932
Library of Congress Control Number: 2008928535

Manuscript edited by: Merrill Furman, Shana Hinds
Design by: Kerry Polite, Polite Design, Philadelphia, Pennsylvania, USA
Printed by: Brilliant Graphics, Exton, Pennsylvania, USA
Press: Heidelberg XL105 Speedmaster
Screening: 300 lpi Heidelberg Hybrid
Paper: NewPage Signature True 100# Gloss Text
Inks: Toyo Process and 11 PMS colors
Bindery: Bindery Associates, Lancaster, Pennsylvania, USA
Font: Interstate; Light, Regular, Bold